THE SAX&BRASS BOOK

BRIAN PRIESTLEY

DAVE GELLY

PAUL TRYNKA

TONY BACON

The Sax & Brass Book
Saxophones, Trumpets and Trombones
in Jazz, Rock and Pop

A BALAFON BOOK

First edition 1998

Published in the United States by Miller Freeman Books
600 Harrison Street, San Francisco, CA 94107
Publishers of *Guitar Player* and *Bass Player* magazines
Miller Freeman, Inc. is a United News and Media company

un Miller Freeman
A United News & Media company

Published in the UK by Balafon Books, an imprint of Outline Press Ltd,
115J Cleveland Street, London W1P 5PN, England.

ISBN 0-87930-531-2

Printed in Hong Kong

Art Director: Nigel Osborne
Design: Sally Stockwell
Photography: Miki Slingsby
Editors: Tony Bacon, John Morrish

Print and origination by Regent Publishing Services

Type formatting and in-house production by Phil Richardson

98 99 00 01 02 5 4 3 2 1

CONTENTS

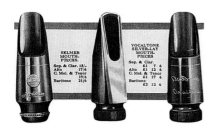

INTRODUCTION

The Sax & Brass Book presents a fresh and exciting view of jazz and pop by blending together the stories of the music, the musicians and their musical instruments into a new and, we hope, stimulating ensemble.

Within these pages you will recognise the great names of the past – from Bix Beiderbecke to Louis Armstrong to Miles Davis, from Coleman Hawkins to Charlie Parker to John Coltrane – all of whom are drawn upon for inspiration and guidance to inform the music of more recent times. But our survey is not limited to jazz, for we have also considered rock, funk, ska, soul, country and more – in fact virtually any popular music that at one time or another has derived strength from the saxophone, the trumpet, the cornet or the trombone.

At the core of The Sax & Brass Book you will find three entertaining and informatively original essays. The first is on the trumpet and trombone in jazz, the second on the saxophone in jazz, and the third on brass instruments in pop music.

Laced in between and around the essays is a unique photographic collection of fine and rare musical instruments and printed memorabilia, especially commissioned and researched for this book. Finally, toward the back of this volume, is a detailed directory of instrument makers that features concise information to help those who wish to understand the background and manufacturing period of key instruments.

We trust that you will enjoy The Sax & Brass Book. We feel sure that it contains new insights, and firmly believe that it will inspire you to visit a wealth of unexplored musical territories.

"With respect to sound, jazz has surely accomplished much of considerable value; it ingeniously transformed what existed for its own tonal style. Through jazz, the piano, the violin, the trumpet and the saxophone have become different instruments. Only the future will show what they seriously have to say."

*EARLY SAX CHAMPION **Jaap Kool** WRITING BACK IN 1931*

"A lot of the musicians asked me if when I hit my high-Cs on the records I had a clarinet take the notes. Some [thought] I had invented some kind of gadget so I could play high register. They weren't satisfied until they handed me a trumpet that they had with them and had me swing it. Then they cheered."

***Louis Armstrong** DOES IT ALL HIMSELF*

"People have said I turn my back [on the live audience] – but it's not like that. On-stage there's always a spot that will register more for the horn player. When I was playing with J.J. Johnson, he used to say 'I'll give you $10 if you let me sit in your spot tonight,' because if it's a good spot for brass, that's where it happens."

***Miles Davis** FINDS THE RIGHT PLACE... DESPITE THE AUDIENCE*

"I was a withdrawn, hypersensitive kid. I would practice the saxophone in the bathroom, and the tenements were so close together that someone from across the alleyways would yell, 'Shut that kid up,' and my mother would say, 'Play louder, Stanley, play louder.'"

*THE POLITICS OF PRACTISING, AS RECALLED BY **Stan Getz***

"Considering the great heritage in music that we have – the work of the giants of the past, the present, and the promise of those who are to come – I feel that we have every reason to face the future optimistically."

***John Coltrane** UNDERSCORES THE FUTURE POSITIVE*

Where "KINGS" are built Acous Correct

THIS PAGE: *The factory of H. N. White in Cleveland, Ohio (above), was first opened in 1909. White produced the King line of brass instruments, making great claims for accuracy of pitch. To that end, the factory installed a "Department of Acoustical Research" (right) under the direction of the founder, Henderson N. White, and his son Richard. It included what was claimed to be the largest set of tuning bells in the world, providing reference pitches for every note on every instrument the company produced.*

OPPOSITE PAGE: *(Top line, left to right) An advertisement in Down Beat magazine celebrates the 1981 return of the Martin saxophone after some years out of production; Leblanc, which bought Holton in 1964, advertises the Holton T101 trumpet in 1991; J.J. Johnson, Kai Winding, Si Zentner, Jiggs Whigham, Will Bradley and Alan Ralph line up for King trombones in 1972. (Middle line, left to right) An Henri Selmer advertisement from Melody Maker in 1930 shows a gold tenor at £39.50 (about $63); Bernard Greerbaum's handsome Christmas 1937 cover for Rhythm magazine; Hawkes & Son of London, forerunners of Boosey & Hawkes, promote the XXth century line of saxophones in 1926. (Bottom Line, left to right) The Spitalny Girls, a quartet of the 1950s, express their allegiance to Reynolds, subsequently merged with the Olds company; Vincent Bach, part of Selmer, advertise the 56 variations on the standard trumpet they offered in 1991; Boosey & Hawkes offer their "Thirty-Two" alto in 1933 at £25.50 (about $41), or a mere £2.55 down (about $4) plus 11 monthly payments.*

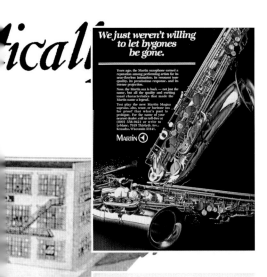

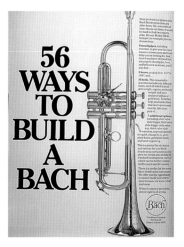

JAZZ TRUMPET AND TROMBONE

by Brian Priestley

Cornet and trumpet players were the first instrumentalists to gain leadership of the early jazz bands, and Louis Armstrong virtually invented the idea of the improvising jazz soloist. Later the saxophone became a stronger voice, but bebop owed much to Dizzy Gillespie, while Miles Davis was never far from the centre of a series of innovative changes in the music, not least the modal schemes and jazz-rock fusion at either end of the 1960s.

IN THE EARLY DAYS OF JAZZ brass instruments played a key role, with none more important than the trumpet and, before that, the cornet. This instrumental authority may have been an inheritance from the line-ups of 19th century military bands and town bands; but whatever the source, trumpets were in charge. Trombones and euphoniums were lower in pitch and so couldn't move around melodically with the same ease, while clarinets and early-model saxophones were musically manoeuvrable but didn't sound as weighty or penetrating.

The trumpet remained as the dominant instrument in jazz until well into the early 20th century, and to most people at the time it epitomised the music. Despite the increasing importance of the saxophone from the 1930s, many of the leading players throughout the history and development of jazz have been trumpeters. Louis Armstrong, Dizzy Gillespie, Miles Davis and Wynton Marsalis are only the most obvious examples not only of musicians who set the style on their instrument but of figureheads of the entire jazz community during their respective eras.

The importance of the trumpet in the African roots of jazz may be because it resembles one of the few wind instruments known in Africa. While the continent is historically associated with percussion and vocal music, conical horns blown to produce a single note existed from ancient times, and relics survived the Atlantic crossing to surface in Haiti and elsewhere. By 1860 or so in a comparatively sophisticated city like New Orleans with an already large black population, trumpeters were apparently a considerable draw in the town's theatres.

They were, of course, playing European music – and the contemporary trumpet is a notable European development. Descended from the relatively primitive bugle which offered a single series of notes ("harmonics") outlining a chord of B-flat, the trumpet became incorporated into symphony orchestras by the 18th century. But despite the harmonic simplicity of European composition at the time, trumpeters still needed a couple of horns pitched in different keys, so composers such as Mozart and Beethoven had to use the trumpet very sparingly. It was only in the 1820s with the addition of three valves, which in combination gave a further six possible key-centres, that the trumpet gained the potential to develop into the virtuoso instrument we know today.

PAWNSHOP PRIZES

A gradual availability of the valve trumpet and an increase in popularity of the B-flat version coincided with the period when brass instruments started to fall into the possession of black musicians. In the late 1860s and 1870s, after the American Civil War and particularly in the defeated Southern states of the

The only known photograph (right) of the first jazz band, led by cornettist Buddy Bolden (standing 2nd right). Next to him is valve-trombonist Willie Cornish. The valve trombone was more common than the slide variety in early New Orleans, because it was standard in US military bands of the period. No drums are visible. No-one knows why the bass and guitar are being held left-handed.

King Master "underslung" cornet c1966 (left) This instrument was owned by the American cornetist Wild Bill Davison. An inscription on its bell records Davison's presentation of the cornet to the British bandleader Alex Welsh "with admiration" in 1967. Welsh died in 1982, and the instrument is presently owned by British cornetist Digby Fairweather. King and Conn were among the leading US makers of cornets. The "underslung" nickname refers to the unusual location of the tuning slide, beneath the valves.

King too was producing a burgeoning line of trumpets alongside its cornet models by 1933, when this ad (right) appeared in the American jazz magazine Metronome, promoting the King Liberty models. The King brand was used by the H.N.White company, based in Cleveland, Ohio.

Butler cornet c1845 (above and left) The cornet was established as a band instrument in the 1830s. This example was built by the British maker George Butler, whose company survived until the 1920s. The extra shanks and crooks seen in the case (left) could be fitted to provide a different basic pitch for the instrument. The coiled crooks for A flat and G died out after about 1850.

King Oliver's Creole Jazz Band (right), the greatest and most influential band of its time, in Chicago in 1923, the year it made its classic recordings. The players are (standing left to right): Baby Dodds (drums), Honore Dutrey (trombone), Bill Johnson (bass), Louis Armstrong (second cornet), Johnny Dodds (clarinet), Lillian Hardin (piano) and, seated, Joe 'King' Oliver (lead cornet). Banjoist Johnny St Cyr is missing. All except Lil were natives of New Orleans. Louis was aged 22. Later he and Lil were married, but she made it a condition of accepting him that he would leave Oliver's band and 'better himself'.

Bix Beiderbecke (left), the first white jazz musician of genius. His bubbling, bright, cheerful solos established the tone of white jazz for generations to come. Bix came from a well-to-do, Mid-Western family, who could never accept their son's choice of profession, even when he became a star of Paul Whiteman's famous orchestra. His best work, however, was recorded with small bands. Bix died a hopeless alcoholic, aged 28, in 1931. A romantic legend of doomed youth soon grew up around his memory.

11

Confederacy, fewer people were playing in military bands and so more instruments were turned over to pawnshops. Black Americans who'd previously been lucky to get their hands on a violin or a homemade guitar now turned to the brass, and in a few prosperous towns such as New Orleans even began to form their own groups, imitating the instrumental line-ups of the standard military bands.

These line-ups also began to appear in most of the official municipal bands, giving the black population a musical style to copy. But for a number of reasons the bands hiring themselves out for black functions soon began to change. Put simply, their secondhand instruments didn't function too accurately, and only a minority of the black musicians of the day could read printed music. So the performers' musicality had to cover up and improve upon these deficiencies. More important was the fact that hints of African styles – already surfacing in piano-based ragtime and the vocal-and-guitar music soon to be known as blues – unconsciously influenced the way the early black brassmen went about their task.

In the late 19th century this all came to a creative head in New Orleans, one of the contributory factors being the city's large number of fraternal societies. Some of these paid the expenses of funeral celebrations, events which always necessitated a band playing solemn spirituals on the way to the burial ground and happy dance-music on the way back. As early New Orleans drummer Zutty Singleton described it, "Right out of the graveyard, the drummer would throw on the snares [previously muffled], roll the drums, get the cats together and light out. The cornet would give a few notes and then, about three blocks from the graveyard, they would cut loose." Singleton's observation, as well as later archive recordings, confirms that the trumpeter or cornetist was already accepted as the leader of every band.

Although all these bands were part-time ventures involving people otherwise employed, often as labourers, there was considerable competition between them. When playing in the streets to advertise a social function for which they were hired, they would often run into another band on a similar mission. This again had the effect of spurring the players to greater resourcefulness and led to the first-known "cutting contests", competitions to see who could play best or longest. New Orleans was also a busy sea-port, with all the entertainment facilities necessary for port workers and off-duty seamen. A huge number of honky-tonks, cabarets, gambling joints and what were known by the genteel name of "sporting houses" (licensed brothels) all provided regular remuneration for musicians. One old-timer recalled that, at a time when an unskilled labourer earned less than $2 a day, "A fellow playing music could make as much as six dollars a night."

BOLDEN BRASS

The roll-call of regularly organised bands active in New Orleans in the early years of the century is a long one, and includes the Onward Brass Band, the Imperial Band, the Olympia Orchestra, Allen's Brass Band, the Melrose Brass Band, the Tuxedo Brass Band, the Superior Orchestra, the Silver Leaf Orchestra, the Maple Leaf Band and the Eagle Band. Most of the small groups in the lower-class joints were less regular and didn't always have names, but the Eagle Band, for instance, was a continuation of the group led by the legendary cornetist Buddy Bolden (1877-1931).

Many stories grew up around the charismatic Bolden: one insisted that on a clear night you could hear his playing on the other side of Lake Pontchartrain, some 20 miles across from New Orleans. Sadly, this imaginative claim is as near as we can get to the real impact of Bolden's sound, since his career ended in 1906 when he was just 28, a good few years before the first "official" jazz recordings. One of Bolden's fellow band members maintained that they'd made records on primitive Edison cylinders, but this too has assumed the quality of legend as no copies have ever been found.

What is significant is that in this undocumented era Buddy's nickname of "King" Bolden carried such weight that all subsequent New Orleans musicians felt obliged to comment on his reputation. For instance, Louis Armstrong later said, "All in all Buddy Bolden was a great musician, but I think he blew too hard. I will even go so far as to say that he did not blow correctly. In any case he finally went crazy." That at least seems to be true, for Bolden is said to have been bedevilled by both alcoholism and syphilis. He was arrested for threatening behaviour while playing in a street parade and, after an intended recuperation, was finally jailed for attacking his mother and mother-in-law. He spent the years from 1907 until his death a quarter-century later confined at the local mental institution, and his crown as the "King" of New Orleans brassmen at first passed to the 13-years-younger Freddie Keppard (1890-1933).

Keppard did make a few records late in his short career. He played in a forthright style that sounded closer to ragtime than classic traditional jazz – rather like Nick LaRocca (1889-1961), cornetist and leader of the Original Dixieland "Jass" Band, the white outfit who were first to make it onto disc. Significantly, Keppard achieved a brief fame by leaving New Orleans and playing in different parts of the US. He found there was a growing audience for this kind of music in California, and also in Chicago where the record industry, previously restricted to New York, was by the 1920s setting up new studios.

But the most important figure of this period was Joe "King" Oliver (1885-1938). He also gained in reputation from travelling out of New Orleans and taking up residence in Chicago. Although five years older than Keppard, Oliver was a slow developer musically and had a less flamboyant style which actually endured better than his predecessors – and in Oliver's case the "King" title stayed with him. Ever after known as King Oliver, Joe was often in dispute with the two Dodds brothers who played clarinet and drums for him. So he maintained discipline on the bandstand by carrying a pistol at all times.

When Oliver was playing the music, however, he had a quiet authority that helped his band of the early 1920s to develop a unified spirit. His own instrumental style made its mark by injecting a healthy dose of the blues, and his poignant muted work was highly regarded, influencing players such as Duke Ellington's first major trumpeter, Bubber Miley (1903-32). Oliver, meanwhile, failed to win a job at New York's Cotton Club which then became a key venue for the young Ellington. After that disappointment, Oliver's career was ruined by the Depression – and along with Keppard and Bolden he died during the 1930s. Stylistically, however, it may be that Oliver had already sealed his fate by 1922 when he invited one Louis Armstrong (1901-71) to be the second cornetist in his band.

When Armstrong travelled from New Orleans to join King Oliver's band in Chicago he was just a few days past his 21st birthday. But he wouldn't have known this. His mother was illiterate and his extremely poor upbringing hadn't allowed for such luxuries as birthday celebrations. When he was put in a children's detention centre at 11 he made up a birthdate of July 4th, but recent research has established that he was born on August 4th 1901. It was the detention centre that provided Armstrong with his only formal tuition on the cornet, but he received further encouragement from Oliver (then still in New Orleans) and from trombonist Kid Ory. Armstrong began to play regularly, sometimes with marching bands, and was already a highly promising player by the time he left his hometown. There was no holding him once he became a member of Oliver's band, who at the time were Chicago's top ensemble of New Orleans exiles (plus one Memphis native, pianist Lil Hardin, who soon became Armstrong's wife).

HOTTER THAN THAT

The classic records of the 1923 Oliver band show a well-balanced ensemble with a typical New Orleans rolling beat and a piquant contrast between the two cornetists. For most of the time Armstrong deliberately plays under the leader, including a couple of duet passages probably influenced by the marching-band repertoire. But when Armstrong briefly plays lead, a different rhythmic feel emerges. The best example is the chorus between Johnny Dodds's clarinet solo and Oliver's famous muted solo on 'Dippermouth Blues' (titled after Armstrong's early nickname, later superseded by Satchelmouth and then the abbreviated Satchmo). Oliver's solo that follows – and indeed the approach of the whole band – has the even-8ths (or straight-quavers) feel of ragtime that was still common at this fast tempo. But Armstrong takes the swing-8ths (or triplet-quavers) style, previously only used on slow blues, and makes it work at speed.

In this way Armstrong set a new rhythmic feel in jazz that predominated during the next four decades, and he did so with an increasingly imperious tone that required all other brass players to imitate him. For just over a year during 1924 and 1925 Armstrong joined the Fletcher Henderson big-band in New York and shook up all the top musicians there, starting with such future greats as Henderson's saxists Don Redman and Coleman Hawkins.

When Armstrong returned to Chicago for the second half of the 1920s he continued working for other bandleaders. But most importantly he began recording under his own name. The series of singles by Louis Armstrong & His Hot Five exposed for the first time his singing, one of the elements that

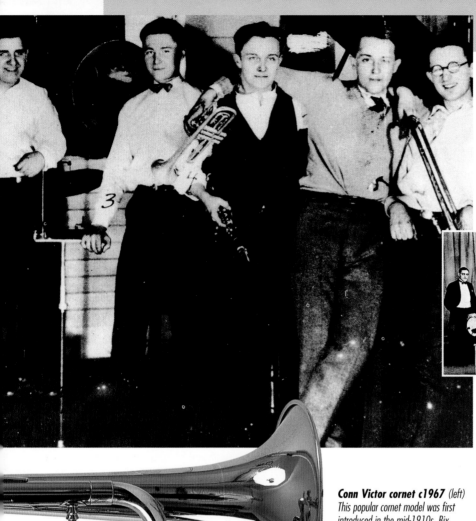

Bix and his Rhythm Jugglers
(left), at Gennett Studios, Richmond, Indiana, on 26 January 1925. Bix is second from right. On extreme right is trombonist Tommy Dorsey, later to become one of greatest bandleaders of the Swing Era. In the background are the giant horns used for acoustic

recording before the advent of microphones. Bix's first regular band, the Wolverines (above), at the Cinderella Ballroom, New York, in September 1924. Bix is far right.

Conn Victor cornet c1967 (left) This popular cornet model was first introduced in the mid-1910s. Bix Beiderbecke's first good instrument was a Conn Victor, which he bought from a fellow high school musician for about

$35. The rotary tuning device of the Victor is nicknamed an "opera glass" tuner because of its resemblance to a focusing wheel. W.C.Handy was another early player of Conn cornets. The Victor was produced for more than 50 years.

CONN'S *latest production!*
The "New Era" Trumpet

IMPROVES YOUR PERFORMANCE

THE SAXOPHONE SHOP LTD., 147, WARDOUR ST.,
LONDON, W.1.

This ad (left), from a 1930 copy of the British musicians' magazine Melody Maker, shows how Conn's trumpets quickly developed alongside its cornets. The model advertised here is the Conn New Era.

Cornettist Muggsy Spanier
(above), renowned for his hot, incisive playing and his authoritative lead in a

Dixieland ensemble. Records by his Ragtimers helped keep the Dixie style alive during the Swing era.

helped them to sell well. However, among the good-natured blues and throw-away pop-songs they all included majestic playing by Armstrong. Some are instrumental classics that will never fade, among them 'Cornet Chop Suey', 'Struttin With Some Barbecue', 'West End Blues' and the duet with pianist Earl Hines, 'Weather Bird'.

While he was in Chicago at this time Armstrong made the definitive switch from cornet to trumpet. (Physically the cornet is similar to the trumpet, differing in the profile of its tubing – the cornet's more conical than the trumpet's cylindrical bore – and the shape of its mouthpiece and throat, and if anything tends to a softer, darker tone.) Armstrong's move to trumpet was justified initially in order to blend better with his section-mates in some of the big-bands he worked with, but the trumpet made his solo work sound even more striking and helped him with high-register playing. This meant that when leading his own band, from the 1930s, he frequently ended tunes with a long series of high Cs and, at the point when exhaustion would have felled a lesser man, he would rise to the previously unattainable top F for a finale. (Unattainable, that is, except for those who played classical music on the outdated baroque trumpet which was actually pitched in F.) While Armstrong later cut down on such acrobatics, and later still in the 1960s severely curtailed his playing in deference to singing, he remained an icon of jazz until his death in 1971.

Despite Armstrong's pre-eminence, the new liberation of solo improvisation he forecast meant that other players were now more free to go their own way. An early example was the famous cornetist Bix Beiderbecke (1903-31), the first truly individual white musician in jazz (even if his reputation during the 1920s was overshadowed by his follower Red Nichols).

At first inspired by the records of the Original Dixieland Band and their leader Nick LaRocca, Beiderbecke had a much less emphatic style than LaRocca – let alone Armstrong – and was more obviously lyrical. Perhaps because he also played very acceptable piano, he played his solo lines more legato – that is with the notes linked together and not so highlighted by their separate articulation – and with a more intimate, appealing tone. As guitarist Eddie Condon described it, "The sound came out like a girl saying yes." Beiderbecke's sound and his legend – he died prematurely in 1931, at the age of 28 – have made him immortal. But despite the major exception of

Beiderbecke, the fact is that Armstrong changed everything. In contrast to the ideal of collective improvisation as typified by the Oliver band and their predecessors, Armstrong pioneered the solo statement and influenced players of completely unrelated instruments such as saxmen Coleman Hawkins and, later, Lester Young and Charlie Parker.

DOWN TO THE BONE

In the late 1920s the previously unwieldy trombone, hitherto restricted in jazz to slow mournful sounds or lower-register burping noises, found a number of executants inspired to follow in Armstrong's footsteps. In many ways they faced a more formidable task than any trumpeter, since the trombone accesses notes in different keys by use of its slide, not by valves. But especially in the upper register, where physics dictates that the notes are closer together, many 'bonists started to create more agile melody lines without breaking their right arms.

One of the first on disc was the white trombonist Miff Mole (1898-1961), recording with the Original Memphis Five as early as 1922. His style matured in the late 1920s on sessions with Red Nichols, both as Miff Mole & His Molers and Red Nichols & His Five Pennies. Mole revealed an impressive jazz technique before he made his move into studio work that included sessions with conductor Arturo Toscanini.

A comparable technical virtuoso was the slightly younger Jimmy Harrison (1900-31) who as a black man found that studio work was not an option. (Apart from a couple of appointments to radio bands for the duration of World War II, black musicians only started to make small inroads into the studio scene in the 1950s and 1960s.) Harrison moved to New York the year before Louis Armstrong, working with Fletcher Henderson among others, but is largely forgotten because he died at the age of 30, of cancer, and made few records.

Harrison's friend and partner during many racially-mixed and therefore unofficial after-hours jam-sessions was the Texan trombonist Jack Teagarden (1905-64). A sure contender for the title of the second great white jazz musician, "Big T" played his instrument with a laidback facility that belied the difficulty of some of his phrases. He had a commanding presence when he played, and shared the black musicians' love of the blues. He also displayed a very natural singing style that helped to make several tunes into standards, including the

14

vocal version of 'Basin Street Blues' (with additional words by Glenn Miller, a would-be jazzer who made a fortune from his less jazzy music). Another future bandleader, Tommy Dorsey (1905-56), equally into jazz in the 1920s, proved to be another excellent technician on the trombone, but always seemed unable to match the natural brilliance of Teagarden. In the slightly improved racial climate brought on by World War II Teagarden was able to tour with and befriend Louis Armstrong.

Armstrong, of course, remained the supreme influence on trumpeters throughout the swing era, a period that lasted about ten years from 1935 and is forever identified with the popular big-bands of Tommy Dorsey, Glenn Miller, Benny Goodman and others. New trumpeters did appear occasionally. Bobby Hackett (1915-76) was one; he sounded a little like Bix Beiderbecke, and in spite of his avowed love of and later engagements with Armstrong he stuck to cornet. But all the other white players who emerged during this period took Armstrong as their main source of inspiration. There was Bunny Berigan (1908-42), who first shone with Goodman on 'King Porter Stomp' and with Dorsey on 'Marie', and Harry James (1916-83) who replaced Berigan in the Goodman band and was notable for his work on both the studio and concert recordings of 'Sing, Sing, Sing'.

As big-bands became a growth industry with the white youth audience of the late 1930s, Berigan, Hackett and James all formed their own units, the first two shortlived but the James outfit untypically lasting through to the 1980s. The black bands already in existence had less access to the white-led swing era market – except indirectly by inspiring white players – and so didn't multiply and subdivide at quite the same rate. The less distinguished of them each had its Armstrong imitator whose job was to copy Satchmo's playing and singing as best as they could. Some bands also developed more specific roles. Jimmie Lunceford first steered his trumpeters Tommy Stevenson (1914-44) and then Paul Webster (1909-66) into becoming high-note specialists, later known in the trade as "screamers". Count Basie's fine outfit featured two contrasting trumpeters: the lyrical Buck Clayton (1911-91) and extrovert Harry "Sweets" Edison (1915-), both deriving from Armstrong but bringing out different aspects of his innovations.

The 1930s band of Duke Ellington was an exceptional case. Its two trumpet soloists were Cootie Williams (1911-85) and Rex Stewart (1907-67), the latter another player who still used the cornet. Both started out as Armstrong admirers but Williams, having been hired as a replacement for the previously-mentioned Bubber Miley, decided to learn Miley's technique of waving a plunger in front of the bell, sometimes growling in his throat at the same time. This rubber plunger (the business end of a drain-clearing device) created such a variable tone that it became possible for the player to sound something like someone talking or singing.

HALF VALVE, HALF HUMAN

Rex Stewart had no need of the plunger for he perfected a "half valve" technique, depressing the valves only half-way to obtain equally humanoid sounds. He also became Ellington's first high-note man, to be superseded in the 1940s by Cat Anderson (1916-81). In passing, it's worth mentioning Ellington's three wildly-contrasting trombone stylists: Tricky Sam Nanton (1904-46) who used the plunger over a *trumpet* straight-mute; Lawrence Brown (1907-) who contributed "open" (unmuted) ballads in the style of Dorsey or Armstrong-like swing; and Juan Tizol (1900-84) who only ever played the eerie, distant-sounding valve-trombone.

The influence of Cootie Williams and Rex Stewart was for a long while limited to members of later Ellington bands, or to the occasional white outfit that imitated Duke's style, such as the Charlie Barnet band. But two key figures emerged from black bands in the 1930s and quickly became responsible for stimulating further developments.

Hot Lips Page (1908-54) was a Texan trumpeter who worked alongside Count Basie for several years before they went (separately) to New York, and his often strident playing and singing were important factors in the growth of what became R&B from the 1940s on. While capable of playing the same style, Roy Eldridge (1911-88) made the first radical advance on the Armstrong method. He admired Armstrong, but Eldridge aimed for the fluency of a saxophone or clarinet coupled with a bristling trumpet tone. By an odd coincidence, these two were briefly featured with famous white bands in the early 1940s: Eldridge with ex-Goodman drummer Gene Krupa; Page with clarinetist Artie Shaw.

Less coincidental is the fact that both were much admired by the young Dizzy Gillespie (1917-93). He too started out as a

15

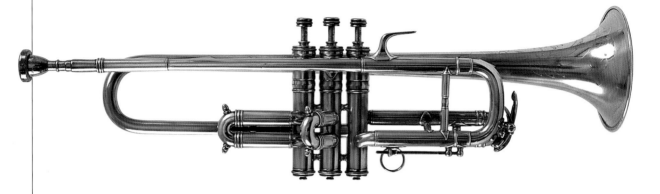

Selmer Louis Armstrong Special trumpet c1933 (above) Selmer Paris netted a publicity coup in 1932 when Louis Armstrong picked up and started to use a new Selmer Challenger trumpet while in London to play at the Palladium. The French company immediately brought out this specially engraved Armstrong model, advertised in a British ad from 1932 (right).

Louis Armstrong first recorded under his own name as leader of the Hot Five (above). This band, purely a recording outfit, contained (left to right) banjoist Johnny St Cyr, Johnny Dodds, his old colleague from King Oliver's band, and trombonist Kid Ory. All were natives of New Orleans. The pianist was Louis's wife, Lil. By the early 1930s (left), Louis had become a rising showbusiness star. His book 'My Life In New Orleans' (right) was meant to be the first volume of his autobiography, but this was never completed.

Count Basie's Octet (left) was formed in 1950, when business got too bad to support his big band. Even so, the Octet was still an all-star affair and beautifully polished, featuring (left to right) Basie on piano, trumpeter Clark Terry, guitarist Freddie Green, Wardell Gray on tenor saxophone, and Buddy De Franco on clarinet. Not shown are drummer Gus Johnson, bassist Rodney Richardson and baritone saxophonist Serge Chaloff. The band's main arranger was Neal Hefti. After two years, Basie formed a new 16-piece line-up and the Octet was disbanded. The big band remained in business for the next three decades, even after Basie's own death in 1984.

Jack Teagarden (left), the Texan trombonist widely regarded as the greatest-ever jazz exponent of his instrument. Too happy-go-lucky to be a successful bandleader, he was a valued member of Louis Armstrong's All-Stars.

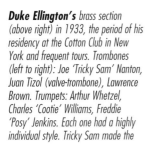

Duke Ellington's brass section (above right) in 1933, the period of his residency at the Cotton Club in New York and frequent tours. Trombones (left to right): Joe 'Tricky Sam' Nanton, Juan Tizol (valve-trombone), Lawrence Brown. Trumpets: Arthur Whetzel, Charles 'Cootie' Williams, Freddie 'Posy' Jenkins. Each one had a highly individual style. Tricky Sam made the trombone shout and snarl, Tizol was warmly romantic, Whetzel was reputed to make listeners cry with his emotional tone and Cootie was king of the growl. In the early 1940s, Cootie left Duke and joined Benny Goodman. amid some recriminations. Later (right) he formed his own successful band, finally returning to Ellington in the 1960s, and staying until Duke's death.

17

big-band trumpeter, joining Teddy Hill and then the famous Cab Calloway. In these formative days Gillespie gradually broke away from the style of Eldridge, who'd been the featured trumpeter in the Hill band himself a couple of years earlier and who already had his own flock of followers. Gillespie's nickname was the standard 1930s way of describing someone who was scatterbrained and a bit of a joker, but those who knew Dizzy Gillespie well realised this was just a front. As singer Billy Eckstine said, "Yeah, he's dizzy – like a fox."

Certainly Gillespie was quite aware that his distinctive tone was thin by comparison with previous players, but at first he paid more attention to obtaining a wide range, and then achieving speed of movement within that range. Diz knew exactly what he was doing, employing a sophisticated harmonic sense to justify unexpected notes in his solos, as well as taking an interest in Afro-Caribbean music which influenced the rhythmic intricacy of his improvisation.

These developments helped Gillespie's involvement in establishing the bebop movement of the 1940s. After jam-sessions with Thelonious Monk at Minton's Playhouse, Gillespie met Charlie Parker and worked alongside him in Earl Hines's band in 1943 and Billy Eckstine's band the following year. Between the two of them, Gillespie and Parker raised the complexity of jazz to new heights, and when they put together their more flexible small groups in the mid 1940s it was apparent that a new style had arrived.

While recordings such as 'Groovin High' and 'Salt Peanuts' were soon accepted as classics, at first they seemed very strange and difficult – not only to the average jazz fan but even to many established musicians. As well as influencing this first phase of bebop, Gillespie furthered his involvement with Afro-Caribbean music, resulting in more exotic pieces like 'A Night In Tunisia', 'Manteca' and others which have been covered by hundreds of performers in the last half-century. The inclusion of a Cuban flavour and a Cuban percussionist in his late-1940s bands led to Gillespie's later concentration on marrying jazz with Latin rhythms like the samba.

Bebop Gillespie

Thanks to Gillespie, bebop influenced the vast majority of subsequent players, even if it was originally seen by the public – even the black public – as a rather cerebral style. Bebop came to have an important effect on dance music, ultimately cross-fertilising with R&B to create the soul-jazz of the 1960s. But one of Gillespie's innovations found few followers, and happened without any deliberate intention. At a party for his wife, Gillespie found that his horn had been accidentally bent out of shape. Checking to find out whether it was still playable, he found he preferred the sound. At the time he endorsed instruments made by the Martin company, so he asked them to build him a trumpet with the bell at a 45-degree angle to the rest of the body. He was unable to patent this modification because something similar had been invented by a French instrument-maker in 1863. But he went on to use the "bent" trumpet until his death in 1993 and when his bands included other trumpeters, such as his young acolyte Jon Faddis (1953-), he insisted that they use such an instrument too.

It was confusing to be a jazz fan in the 1940s. Along with the creative force of bebop and the considerable popular success of the equally new R&B came the Dixieland revival. Sparked off by the work of the King Oliver-influenced white cornetist Muggsy Spanier (1906-67) it soon unearthed a whole generation of New Orleans musicians still playing this type of music. Enthusiasm for the music then inspired many younger musicians, especially in Europe where trumpeters such as Humphrey Lyttelton (1921-), Ken Colyer (1928-88) and Kenny Ball (1930-) with trombonist Chris Barber (1930-) ensured the lasting popularity of what became known as "trad" jazz. In the US Bunk Johnson (1889-1949), an unrecorded trumpeter born two months before pioneer Freddie Keppard, became a figurehead – but only after being provided with a new set of false teeth – while trombonist Kid Ory (1886-1973) was rediscovered after several years of running a chicken farm.

All these changes were also confusing to musicians, especially those who played the trombone. Few innovators had come along during the swing era, except perhaps the Count Basie sideman Dicky Wells (1907-85) who in a wittily eccentric manner combined an extreme upper-register facility with the sliding noises available from the instrument. The white trombonist Bill Harris (1916-73) had emerged during the swing era but became particularly identified with the bebop-influenced band of Woody Herman, and purveyed similar eccentricities with a rougher tone, as did Danish-born Kai Winding (1922-83) in the Stan Kenton band. Both Harris and

Winding occasionally used the valve-trombone, especially in small bebop groups where greater mobility was required, but the only musician permanently to adopt this instrument more recently was Bob Brookmeyer (1929-). The flamboyant high-note trumpeter Maynard Ferguson (1928-) had surfaced in the late 1940s and occasionally played the valve-trombone for a change of pace. Later, during the 1970s, Ferguson designed with the Holton company his "superbone" which combined valve and slide facilities in a single instrument.

J.J. Johnson (1924-) proved that the slide-trombone could attain sufficient rapidity of articulation to be used in bebop. Beginning in the mid 1940s and still active today, he understood the bebop language and adapted it to the instrument, gradually leaving behind what at first was a stilted delivery and going on to achieve an impressive maturity by the late 1950s. Before that he ran a popular two-trombone group with Kai Winding for a couple of years, during which time they both dabbled with a trombone/euphonium hybrid called, naturally enough, the trombonium. From the 1960s Johnson benefited from the relaxation of racial barriers in the studio world, becoming a busy session man and then a composer and musical director for film and television.

An honourable mention should also be made of two white trombone players first heard in the 1950s, Jimmy Knepper (1927-) and Willie Dennis (1926-65), who each worked with Charles Mingus and achieved amazing mobility without using the rapid-fire staccato tonguing employed by Johnson. But it was undoubtedly Johnson who became the leading influence on young jazz trombonists.

MILES AND THE COOL

The expanded horizons of bebop opened up yet more variants of trumpet style, in the same way that Armstrong had liberated the players of 20 years before. Two trumpeters who exerted a considerable long-term effect despite their tragically premature deaths were Fats Navarro (1923-50) and Clifford Brown (1930-56).

Navarro was six years younger than Gillespie, and followed him into the Billy Eckstine band (as Gillespie had succeeded Eldridge with Teddy Hill). Navarro proved to be a highly adequate replacement. The half-Cuban trumpeter created lines that were less rhythmically varied but beautifully melodic, in

contrast to the more angular style of Gillespie, with a more conventionally full tone than Dizzy and a range almost as extensive. Navarro died in 1950 at the age of 26. Clifford Brown didn't even reach 26: he'd been recording for a mere three years when he met his end in a car accident. Brownie was, if anything, more promising than Fats, and his style – typified by his tune and subsequent improvisation on 'Joy Spring' – remains a benchmark for players today.

Then there was Miles Davis (1926-91). He burst on the scene early, sitting in with Dizzy Gillespie and Charlie Parker in the Eckstine band before he turned 18. On only his second record session, at 19, he performed a couple of striking solos with the great Parker. Although briefly inspired by Gillespie, Davis soon discovered the virtue of playing within the limitations of his own tone and technique, which were dramatically different to Dizzy's. It was like the contrast between Louis Armstrong and his contemporary Bix Beiderbecke, whose tone and approach sounded introverted next to Armstrong. At a time when every other young trumpeter was trying to sound as much as possible like Dizzy, Miles was more lyrical, more legato and more obviously melodic. Also like Bix, Miles was at first overshadowed. In the early and mid 1950s the success of Chet Baker (1929-88) eclipsed Miles, even if Baker's whole trumpet style and, later, much of his repertoire was based on Davis's achievements. But Miles proved to have greater staying power, as well as the ability to reinvent himself continuously during a career that would last nearly 50 years.

Davis had enough vision and charisma to be able repeatedly to assemble casts of collaborators who together created new styles and set new standards for the rest of the jazz world to follow. In the modest words of Miles himself, "I changed the music about five or six times." This was certainly true.

The first example was his late-1940s "Birth Of The Cool" group that established a new "cool" jazz, artfully scored and a calmer contrast to the hurried rhythms of bebop. There followed in 1955-57 Davis's group featuring saxophonist John Coltrane, heard on *Round About Midnight* and other albums, and then the 1958-59 group with Coltrane and Cannonball Adderley which made the classic *Kind Of Blue*. This could have been subtitled the "Birth Of Modal Jazz" as it heralded a new freedom in improvisation, this time departing from the dictates of backing harmonies by using scales, or modes, rather

H.N. White continued to aim their
King Silver Flair trumpet at jazz
musicians, as this 1966 ad (above)
from jazz magazine Down Beat
demonstrates. Dizzy Gillespie used a
Silver Flair as well as his Martin.

Dizzy Gillespie had his creative
heyday in the 1940s, when he laid
down the foundations of bebop and
toured with his big band (top). The
pianist is John Lewis and the bassist
Ray Brown, later members of the
original Modern Jazz Quartet. This was
before he had discovered the trumpet
with the upturned bell, as featured in
this advertisement for Martin (above).
On one of his last visits to Britain, in
the late 1980s (below), he used a
radio-microphone in the bell of his
trumpet. Although no longer reaching
the topmost reaches of the trumpet, he
still played with great authority.

This Martin trumpet (above) once
belonged to Dizzy Gillespie. It features
the upturned bell that became his
trademark, originally caused when
someone fell on his instrument at a
party. Dizzy tried it, and discovered he
preferred the sound. He used only bent-
bell instruments from then on.

Bach Stradivarius trumpet c1998 (below) Vincent Bach was an Austrian-born trumpet player who moved to the United States at the start of World War I in 1914. Bach became interested in the mechanics of his instrument, and began to make mouthpieces (see 1950 ad, inset). Then in 1924 Bach began making trumpets and cornets. The company's Stradivarius trumpet is acclaimed by many players, and while classical players took readily to the instrument, jazz musicians were not slow in picking up Bach instruments; the talented jazz trumpeter Clifford Brown (see photo, right) was one such Bach player. In 1953 Bach moved from their original base in New York City to Mount Vernon, New York. The company was sold to Selmer in 1961. The new Stradivarius shown here is silver-plated, but otherwise differs from the 1924 original only in minor details.

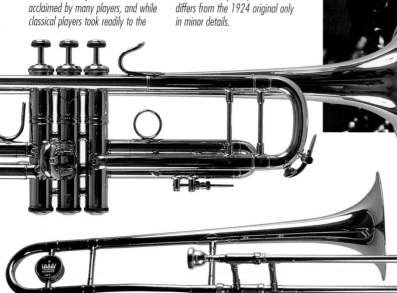

Clifford Brown (above) on stage with the band he co-led with drummer Max Roach from 1954 until his death two years later at the age of 26. His front-line partner on tenor saxophone is the great Sonny Rollins.

21

King trombone c1996 (above) The Cleveland, Ohio, based H.N. White company had started their King brand of instruments by making trombones back in 1893 after collaborating with a local trombonist called Thomas King. Later, the King brand would be used for saxophones, trumpets and all manner of brass instruments, and as this example indicates, King instruments are still in production today. The brand is now owned by United Musical Instruments.

J.J. Johnson (right) was the first trombonist to develop a technique fast and accurate enough to master the intricacies of bebop. A member of the Benny Carter band at the age of 18, he made his first impact on records with Charlie Parker in 1947. In the 1950s he led a two-trombone quintet with Kai Winding, called Jay & Kai, which showed off to perfection their amazing agility. His tone has blossomed and ripened with the passing years and he has recorded as a soloist with such leading composers as Andre Previn and Robert Farnon. Johnson is a talented composer himself, with a number of film scores to his credit.

than conventional chord sequences. Between the last two Davis also started a series of big-band recordings with arranger Gil Evans, including *Porgy And Bess*, and these too set in motion influences still heard around the world today.

Davis was not only an innovator in group styles, but also in his own sound. He realised early on that while his tone on the instrument was unbrass-like and melancholic, this was in fact a potential advantage that could be exploited. With his very personal articulation, he set about making it more attractive. One way of doing so in the early 1950s, especially on slow ballads, was to play with a cup mute, but Davis's tone became much more intriguing when in 1954 he discovered the harmon mute. Like the cup mute this had been around since the 1860s, but its metal body with an adjustable central stem provided a sharper edge to the muted sound than other such devices. Miles made it even more edgy by removing the stem altogether and placing the muted bell of the instrument close to a microphone to make it sufficiently audible.

But Davis still hadn't finished his sound innovations. In 1957 and 1958, on the *Miles Ahead* album with Gil Evans and on the title track of *Milestones*, his "open" (unmuted) work was often played on a flugelhorn. This instrument, of the same pitch as the trumpet and cornet, had previously been used by only a handful of jazzmen, including Davis's mentor Clark Terry (1920-), one of the first bebop-inclined musicians to find a home in the Ellington band of the 1950s. The flugel's more rounded tone became extremely popular thanks to Miles and has generally replaced the cornet for jazz trumpeters who wish to double on an extra instrument.

It became virtually impossible for most young players to escape the influence of Miles during this period of his career. As with earlier role models, however, one or two players who emerged as followers went on to display their own individuality. The underrated Kenny Dorham (1924-72), who followed Davis into Charlie Parker's group, actually started out as a Gillespie imitator but showed a distant Miles influence in his excellent work of the 1950s and 1960s.

FARMER'S FLUMPET

Nat Adderley (1931-), brother of the aforementioned Cannonball, can turn on a convincing imitation of Davis even today, but has aspects of Clark Terry and others in his playing,

and except in big-bands he uses a cornet. Also still active is Art Farmer (1928-). He toured with both Horace Silver and Gerry Mulligan in the 1950s, has a more poignant tone even than Miles, and since the 1960s concentrated on the flugel for his solos. But a few years ago Farmer asked custom instrument-maker Dave Monette to build him a "flumpet" – a cross between a flugelhorn and a trumpet – of which he is so far the chief exponent.

The late 1950s proved to be a period of consolidation for bebop – and of hard times for many older musicians. Some, such as Buck Clayton and Rex Stewart, were frequently reduced to abandoning their own styles and playing the trad repertoire, while Cootie Williams was leading an R&B band. Much to everyone's surprise – and to his own economic disadvantage – a young white cornetist named Ruby Braff (1927-) arrived with a swing-based style which he still espouses today. Especially after the tragic demise of Clifford Brown, the time seemed ripe for performers who sought to combine the verve of Brown with some of the depth of Davis. Two precociously talented youngsters obliged.

Lee Morgan (1938-72) in particular got off to a flying start, working in Gillespie's big-band at 18 and making a host of small-group albums before he was 20, at which time he joined drummer Art Blakey. His contemporary Freddie Hubbard (1938-), three months older, was only slightly slower in moving to New York, recording with Cannonball Adderley and Coltrane and replacing Morgan in Blakey's Jazz Messengers.

In the 1960s, Morgan and Hubbard each had to come to terms with a new split in the jazz world, recalling the developments of the 1940s. While older musicians such as Clayton and Stewart and the young Braff pursued a swing revival under the guise of "mainstream" jazz, there was a striking new approach typified by saxophonist Ornette Coleman, usually described as free jazz or avant-garde.

Meanwhile the bebop players risked losing out in the same way as the swing players had 15 years earlier. Some at least aligned themselves with popular dance music – more akin to the start of R&B – and generated a new style known as soul-jazz. Morgan and Hubbard each had successes in this field, Morgan with the title-track of his album *The Sidewinder* and Hubbard with *Backlash*, though both of them also continued to play in a post-bebop style touched with avant-garde trimmings. Morgan was shot dead at the age of 33, while Hubbard has in recent years been plagued by severe problems with embouchure (the condition and relationship of the player's lips and mouth to the instrument).

Don Cherry (1936-95) was the chief architect of the trumpet style within free jazz, and had arrived spectacularly as saxophonist Ornette Coleman's front-line partner. Cherry grew up with bebop leanings, but Coleman's approach, like Miles's modal jazz, disposed of the chord sequences which had underpinned all jazz improvisation from Louis Armstrong onwards. This liberation allowed Cherry to create lively solos, sounding rather as Miles might have done in his early years had bebop not been the dominant style. It also enabled Cherry, like Miles, to triumph over a fairly limited technique. Cherry made use of a miniature cornet built by the French firm Besson; he called it his "pocket trumpet". Throughout the 1960s he travelled widely and involved musicians from many different backgrounds including European, Turkish, Asian, South American and South African. He also started to collect and play various ethnic flutes, string instruments and percussion, and became a pioneer of jazz and world music fusions until his death in 1995.

Cherry started working at a time when music in the free jazz style (and in the simultaneous soul-jazz movement) had almost imperceptibly begun to move away from the swing feel brought to prominence by Louis Armstrong, back toward the even-8ths feel common to ragtime, Latin and other exotic musics. As a result the rhythmic style of the free players was loosened up such that they felt able to switch at will between different implied rhythms – or indeed to no rhythm at all in some of their more rhapsodic moments. Among the trumpeters who asserted their own styles within the free area are two who first surfaced during the 1960s, Leo Smith (1941-), who also features some ethnic instruments, and Lester Bowie (1940-) of the Art Ensemble of Chicago, latterly known for his more popular Brass Ensemble.

Few trombonists were equally individual in their work, although the free style did give them the necessary licence to exploit fully the weird-sounding potential of the slide mechanism. As often seems the case with this instrument some of the more renowned practitioners were white, one of the most notable being Roswell Rudd (1935-). Like certain other free

jazzers he started out as a trad player and made the transition in one jump, missing completely what's been called the "slide denial" of bebop trombone.

Bebop was, however, the background of Albert Mangelsdorff (1928-), who attained an international reputation while remaining based in his native Germany. Part of his expertise lies in the use of "multiphonics", a technique available on all reed and brass instruments but perhaps most effective with the wider embouchures of trombone and tuba. It involves altering the air pressure or the position of the lips to produce two or more notes simultaneously, or playing one note while singing another to produce a third as the harmonics interact.

BITCHES BREW

When jazz improvisation was freed from a strict adherence to chord sequences, and rhythm was loosened by a shift to even-8ths, several established players reacted creatively – in particular Miles Davis. His quintet of 1963-69 with pianist Herbie Hancock, bassist Ron Carter, drummer Tony Williams and (from 1964) saxophonist Wayne Shorter became a kind of research laboratory for the study of the effect that these changes were having on the standard bebop format.

Some of the results were displayed on the albums *Miles Smiles* and *ESP*, and the combination of modal, free and rhythmic influences has acted as a guide for many musicians since, as has the more direct fusion style of the early 1970s when Miles began to absorb the impact of electric rock and funk bands. The attempts of musicians with a rock background to expand the brass section in groups such as Chicago and Blood Sweat & Tears paled beside Davis's growing interest in Sly & The Family Stone and Jimi Hendrix, demonstrated by the music on his *Bitches Brew* and *Live-Evil* albums.

Miles's own playing remained identifiably his own, even if he did listen with approval to the early Don Cherry. But its setting changed dramatically as his rhythm section incorporated first an electric bass, then electric keyboards (often two or three players simultaneously) and eventually electric guitarists. This made it logical for the trumpet itself to be wired up, and by the start of the 1970s Davis was into a new phase of innovation for his trumpet sound. Partly this occurred because of the availability of portable effects units such as echo, ring modulator and wah-wah pedal. Apart from replacing the

Miles Davis (left, 1950s) stayed in the forefront of jazz innovation from the moment he arrived on the New York scene at age 19. The 1950s saw his popularity climb to pop-star levels, making Miles the natural choice for the cover of Metronome magazine's 1961 Trumpet Special (below).

Jazz brass players have always altered their sound by applying such things as cups, hats and sink plungers to the bell of the instrument. Gradually, a range of custom-made mutes evolved, a typical example being the versatile Harmon (right), which has a chamber with a moveable tube, which can be extended or removed altogether. Miles Davis introduced a new sound when he played through a Harmon with the tube removed, directly into a microphone.

Martin Committee trumpet c1997 (above) So-called because it was designed by a committee of players, Martin's Committee became a firm favourite among jazz players in the 1950s, not least Miles Davis (1962 ad, left), who used one throughout most of his career. Martin was bought by Leblanc in 1971. This recent Committee exhibits some modern design changes.

Besson flugelhorn c1997 (above right) The flugelhorn resembles the trumpet, but with a wider bore and bell for a fuller tone. Miles Davis used a Besson flugelhorn for his "open" (unmuted) work of the late 1950s, including 'Miles Ahead' and the title track of 'Milestones'. Besson originated in France in the 1830s, and was bought by Boosey & Hawkes in 1948. The 1957 ad (above) lists Davis as a Besson player.

Jazz-rock-fusion was largely the creation of Miles Davis (right), who changed his own visual style as radically as he revolutionised jazz itself. Although he was approaching 50, with great achievements behind him, he refused to look back. As he changed, many of his former fans gave up trying to follow him, but he gained a whole new audience at rock festivals and venues such as the Fillmore. In the 1980s his band featured such contemporary figues as Marcus Miller and Daryl 'The Munch' Jones and embraced synthesized sound, with Miles himself doubling on keyboards.

Miles Davis produced some of the most influential albums in jazz history, as both player and bandleader. 'Kind of Blue' (top) introduced the listening public to modal improvisation. 'Bitches Brew' (above) was a key text of the early jazz-rock fusion movement.

25

leads attached to his instrument with the wireless pickups that became available in the 1980s, Davis maintained this approach amid a rock-influenced group sound until his death in 1991.

TAKE THIRTY-TWO

Naturally these radical departures within Miles's style found an echo among some other established players. Don Ellis (1934-78) was initially involved in free jazz, but by the late 1960s had studied Indian and other exotic musics and incorporated rock influences and amplification into his bands. The most memorable side effect of these experiments was Ellis's use of complex meters, not merely five or seven beats to the bar (already explored by the likes of Max Roach and Dave Brubeck) but time signatures such as 19 and 32, the latter subdivided into frighteningly irregular groupings. Ellis's interest in Asian music also led him to obtain a trumpet with a fourth valve, enabling the production of quarter-tones that fall between conventionally Westernised semitones. Trumpet amplification became relatively commonplace, but few went so far as free-jazz trombonist George Lewis (1952-) who combined live playing with synthesiser modification.

While many of Miles's contemporaries were automatically hostile to the integration of rock elements into jazz, many younger players were naturally open to his apparent legitimisation of jazz-rock fusions. Randy Brecker (1945-) and Lew Soloff (1944-) played in succession with Blood Sweat & Tears in the late 1960s, later moving to prolific session work. Although they were dedicated to keeping up their jazz playing with acoustic bands, when leading their own groups they found it natural to incorporate influences from rock music and to use electronic manipulation of their instrumental sound. The same was true, at least during the 1970s, of trumpeter Eddie Henderson (1940-), first noted as a member of Herbie Hancock's post-Davis sextet. However, like both Brecker and Soloff, Henderson has tended to emphasise a more conventional post-bebop style since then.

This return to the values of pre-electric jazz was already gaining ground during the 1970s, and became particularly audible in the work of Woody Shaw (1944-89). When he too took the chair of Lee Morgan and Freddie Hubbard in the Jazz Messengers there was already considerable use of electric bass and keyboards in that band, as indeed there would be on his

own later records. But despite being almost exactly the same age as Brecker and Soloff, Shaw declined to amplify his trumpet (other than with a conventional microphone set-up).

Shaw's own playing was far from traditional. Going further than Hubbard, he combined an articulation derived from Clifford Brown with a language from saxophonist John Coltrane (and that second example underlines the fact that the trumpet was no longer setting the style for other instruments). However, especially after working with senior saxophonist Dexter Gordon, Shaw was responsible for leading a move back to the more traditional quintet and sextet line-ups of bebop while continuing to create new material. Another portent during this period was the growing international reputation of British-based Kenny Wheeler (1930-) who, through work with saxophonist Anthony Braxton and others, demonstrated a further, purely acoustic, post-Coltrane trumpet style.

But Wheeler's influence was limited by geography, and in 1989 Shaw became yet another significant trumpeter to die prematurely, at the grand old age of 44. Long before that, Shaw had seen his potential role as a figurehead filled by an exceptional newcomer, Wynton Marsalis (1961-), who was 15 years his junior. Yet another in the long and distinguished line of Jazz Messengers, which he had joined at the age of 18, Marsalis found himself in the right place at the right time.

Marsalis was immediately recognised by fellow players as a truly gifted musician but, surrounded by a growing appetite for a return to acoustic jazz, he received unprecedented promotion from the record industry and from journalists. The nearest equivalent in the past to his media profile was Chet Baker, whose career and individuality had been totally overwhelmed by the process. Marsalis, however, has been able to survive both the promotion and the inevitable backlash.

Supremely articulate, Marsalis has made sometimes ill-judged comments about others – criticising, for example, Miles's attempts at fusion – but these must be balanced against his beneficial effect on the general public's perception of jazz. Ironically, the music first associated with Marsalis's own groups, on albums such as Father Time and Think Of One, was derived very clearly from Miles's pre-fusion quintet style of 1963-69, to which Marsalis brought his own special flair. Since then, his vision has broadened retrospectively, with an appreciation of the trad jazz heritage of his hometown, New

Orleans, and the trumpet tradition of Duke Ellington's orchestra, as heard on *The Majesty Of The Blues*. Of course, Marsalis has yet to absorb all of the innovative jazz that existed prior to fusion, yet hints of everything up to John Coltrane and Ornette Coleman can be detected in his music.

It's ironic, therefore, that misguided detractors of his apparently backward-looking stance describe Marsalis as "playing bebop". The comment is perhaps more true of some of the projects of Roy Hargrove (1970-), one of Marsalis's most talented younger discoveries, but as always with stylistic revivals the music has been considerably changed by the unintentional influence of events in the intervening years. In any case, most of those who are still thought of as the Marsalis school – such as Terence Blanchard (1962-), Nicholas Payton (1973-), Russell Gunn and others – have their own differing views of their position in relation to the history of jazz. When not sounding too much like Marsalis himself, they demonstrate their own individual promise of things to come.

KING OF THE JAZZ BRASS

No comparable developments have taken place among trombonists and, as at times in the past, they are often ready to take up an additional horn or alternative techniques to enhance their work. A unique contemporary trombonist is Steve Turré (1948-), who first appeared with multi-saxophonist Rahsaan Roland Kirk and Woody Shaw in the late 1970s. Since then Turré has added variety by specialising in conch-shells, producing with a suitable embouchure musical sounds from the holes on the surface of "instruments" found on the seashore that require none of the craftsmanship of professional manufacturers. If Turré's playing catches on, maybe there will be a line of them available in music stores.

Several other members of the brass family have found their interpreters in the jazz field. The French horn has occasionally been able to transcend its sluggish articulation and its distant, veiled tone, which are of course distinct disadvantages for jazz improvisation. Although more often used as part of a large brass section in a big-band format, the French horn was successfully played in the bebop style by Julius Watkins (1921-77) who recorded memorably with Thelonious Monk and Charles Mingus as well as doing session work. More recently, agile soloists in post-bebop contexts have included John Clark

(1944-) and Tom Varner (1957-), who studied with Watkins.

The mellophone, similar in sound to the French horn but easier to play, was used as a double in the 1950s by trumpeter Don Elliott (1926-84) before he became a percussion and vocal specialist. A variant produced in the 1950s by Conn was the mellophonium, its bell pointing forwards instead of upwards. It was incorporated into Stan Kenton's big-band of the 1960s, but did not produce any distinguished soloists.

The same rapid dismissal should not be made in the case of the tuba family, although use of the euphonium (technically a tenor tuba) has been fairly limited in jazz. More usually heard is the bass tuba which was often employed in early jazz outfits as a rhythm instrument before the ascendancy of the string double-bass. (Sometimes a sousaphone, named after but not invented by bandmaster John Philip Sousa and with its body encircling the performer's chest, fulfilled this brass-bass role.)

The tuba later distinguished itself thanks to the inspiration of more melodic double-bassists, through the writing of arranger Gil Evans. It can be heard, for instance, on the Miles Davis tracks 'The Duke' and 'Buzzard Song' from *Miles Ahead* and *Porgy And Bess* respectively. Bill Barber (1920-) was the session man who played these demanding parts, and he inspired others to improvise on the instrument.

But the tuba and indeed the trombone are unlikely to unseat the trumpet as king of the jazz brass instruments. And even though Wynton Marsalis has instigated a reassessment of jazz history and inspired a host of followers, it does of course remain difficult to predict new stylistic developments, and as ever it seems unwise to assume that the last word has been said on the subject. Nor is it true to say that all young trumpeters now automatically take the Marsalis view of the music, for the recent revived interest in free jazz has brought to light several promising players, such as Dave Douglas and Ron Miles.

The worst-case scenario might be that contemporary musicians become so tied up in their attempts to replicate the past that they fail to spark fresh interest by introducing innovations or new combinations of ideas. But those attempts to copy old styles are in any case always doomed to failure, and new ideas within established traditions tend to come about without planning or forethought. If all else fails, there are endless lessons to be learnt through studying in detail the work of earlier exponents – and endless pleasure to be gained too.

Blessing Artist mellophonium c1978 (below) The earlier mellophone, as played by Don Elliot (right), had a bell that faced the ground, but later Conn and other makers came up with this variant called the mellophonium, an instrument with a forward-facing bell. Consequently the mellophonium was a slightly more portable and practical instrument, and one that was also more suitable for stage and bandstand performances. However, it has found few notable jazz applications — although the Stan Kenton band of the early 1960s did feature briefly a four-piece mellophonium section.

Don Elliot (1926-84), a rare jazz exponent of the mellophone and winner of the 'miscellaneous instrument' section in numerous jazz polls. The instrument is widely used in US marching bands as a substitute for the more difficult French horn.

Trumpeter Wynton Marsalis (below and right) is one of the most remarkable prodigies in the history of jazz. Born in 1961, the son of pianist Ellis Marsalis, he began playing at age six. At 14 he played the Haydn Trumpet Concerto with the New Orleans Philharmonic and at 18 he joined Art Blakey's Jazz Messengers. Hailed as both the greatest classical and jazz trumpet player of his generation, he also directs the jazz programme at New York's Lincoln Center and its full-time jazz repertory orchestra.

JUMP START AND JAZZ
WYNTON MARSALIS

DOWN BEAT
Jazz, Blues & Beyond

September 1990, $1.95 U.K. £2.25

WYNTON
ON
Ellington
2 Live Crew
Miles
Sesame Street
& More
(Whew!)

N!
ON TH
M
WILLIAMS
DB '90 Hall of Fame Inductee
JOHN HIATT
BLUES FEST,
Chicago Style

WYNTON MARSALIS' HORN OF PLENTY
Twenty-year old Wynton Marsalis is one of the most talked about trumpeters in years:
"As a jazz soloist, he is a symbol for the new decade." —Leonard Feather/L.A. Times
"Wynton Marsalis is the most remark-able musician to appear on the scene in quite some time!" —Ron Carter
"(in concert) Marsalis' mulled and open horn was dynamite, his use of space and notes impressive... played with impeccable time." —down beat
That's why veterans like Herbie Hancock, Ron Carter and Tony Williams have joined Wynton on his debut album. And why you should too.
WYNTON MARSALIS
"WYNTON MARSALIS" THE DEBUT ALBUM.

Marsalis released his debut album, Horn Of Plenty, at age 20. Since then he has created and recorded major works, such as his jazz oratorio Blood On The Fields.

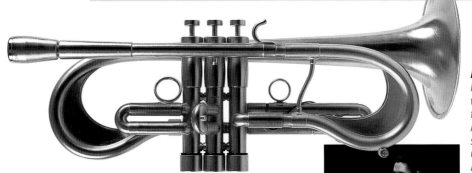

Monette Flumpet c1997 (left) Art Farmer was a jazz flugelhorn player who was inspired to return to the trumpet when he started to play a Monette. Subsequently Farmer, who since the 1940s has played with Clifford Brown, Horace Silver, Gerry Mulligan, Kenny Clarke and in his own outfits, collaborated with David Monette to design the "flumpet", ostensibly a cross between a flugelhorn and a trumpet. Guy Barker (left), who owns the Monette Flumpet pictured here, describes its sound as darker than a trumpet and almost horn-like.

Britain's Guy Barker (right) was born in Britain in 1957 and is one of the leading trumpeters of his generation. Like Wynton Marsalis, he has immersed himself in the jazz tradition and can work successfully in many idioms. He has played in Beiderbecke tributes and alongside Ornette Coleman as well as leading his own successful quintet.

Monette Raja trumpet c1995 (above) David Monette's company is based in Portland, Oregon, and produces some of the finest modern handmade trumpets. The gold-plated Raja trumpet — this example is owned by British musician Guy Barker (pictured above, right) — was developed by Monette in the late 1980s, and is unusual not only in its modern styling but also because it has an integral mouthpiece, and weighs much more than a regular trumpet.

Roy Hargrove was born in 1969 and is pictured (above) on the sleeve of his 1995 album, Family, with his Inderbinen flugelhorn. Hargrove is a high-energy hard-bopper who sides with Marsalis in the anti-fusion debate.

Wallace Roney (above) is a year younger than Hargrove and is generally considered the finest trumpeter of his generation after Marsalis. This 1990 LP, Obsession, includes drummer Cindy Blackman and saxman Gary Thomas.

Nicholas Payton (above) was born in New Orleans, and this 1997 album pitched the 22-year-old trumpet/ flugelhorn prodigy with bassist Christian McBride and guitarist Mark Whitfield to celebrate the music of Herbie Hancock.

JAZZ SAXOPHONE

by Dave Gelly

It was Coleman Hawkins who first defined the saxophone's role in jazz, turning it from a hooting, ineffective horn into the music's leading solo voice. All manner of distinctive accents coloured that voice – from the romantic Johnny Hodges to the indelicate bebop of Charlie Parker, the commanding John Coltrane to the frenetic free jazz of Ornette Coleman – so that today no other instrument rivals the sax at the expressive heart of jazz.

THE FIRST REAL JAZZ SAXOPHONIST of note was Sidney Bechet (1897-1959), the New Orleans clarinet virtuoso. Bechet bought a soprano saxophone in London in 1919 while on tour with Will Marion Cook's Southern Syncopated Orchestra. Almost immediately he began to use the new instrument in his feature-numbers with Cook's band. His playing revealed the saxophone's curious tendency to sound not like itself, but like the person playing it.

Bechet was a forceful and dominant personality with a florid, passionate musical style. When he played the soprano saxophone it sounded exactly that way; the tone was thick, the vibrato was wide, and the volume was loud enough to drown out all opposition. In 1924, when they were both young men, Bechet and Louis Armstrong recorded together as members of a scratch band called The Red Onion Jazz Babies, and the session is notable as very probably the only occasion in his entire recorded career when Armstrong sounds as though he has met his match.

Despite Bechet's example – or more likely because of it – jazz saxophonists shied away from the soprano for many years. Only after Bechet's death in 1959 was it really taken up again in a big way. But the man more often credited with inventing the saxophone as a jazz instrument is Coleman Hawkins

(1904-69). When Hawkins began recording with Fletcher Henderson's orchestra in 1924 the saxophone – particularly the tenor – simply did not have a voice. It hooted away harmlessly in dance bands, but any attempt at soloing seemed doomed from the start and resulted in a rubbery gurgle interspersed with the occasional damp belch.

At first, as a teenage member of Mamie Smith's Original Jazz Hounds, Hawkins sounded much like all the others, although he could nip around the instrument with more facility than most. And like everyone else he relied heavily on the violent, popping attack known as "slap-tonguing". It was after he had joined Henderson that the first glimmerings of his true style began to appear. Nevertheless, almost until the close of the 1920s his playing had the typically awkward, lumbering gait and aimless phrasing of all early saxophonists.

Then, at the end of 1929, he turned up at a recording session with the Mound City Blue Blowers, a "novelty" band that featured singer Red McKenzie on comb-and-paper. Hawkins played a solo on a tune called 'Hello Lola', the echoes of which are still reverberating today. No one had ever heard before a tenor saxophone played with such fluency or agility and with such a confident, mature voice. The other number recorded by the Blue Blowers that day was the ballad 'If I Could

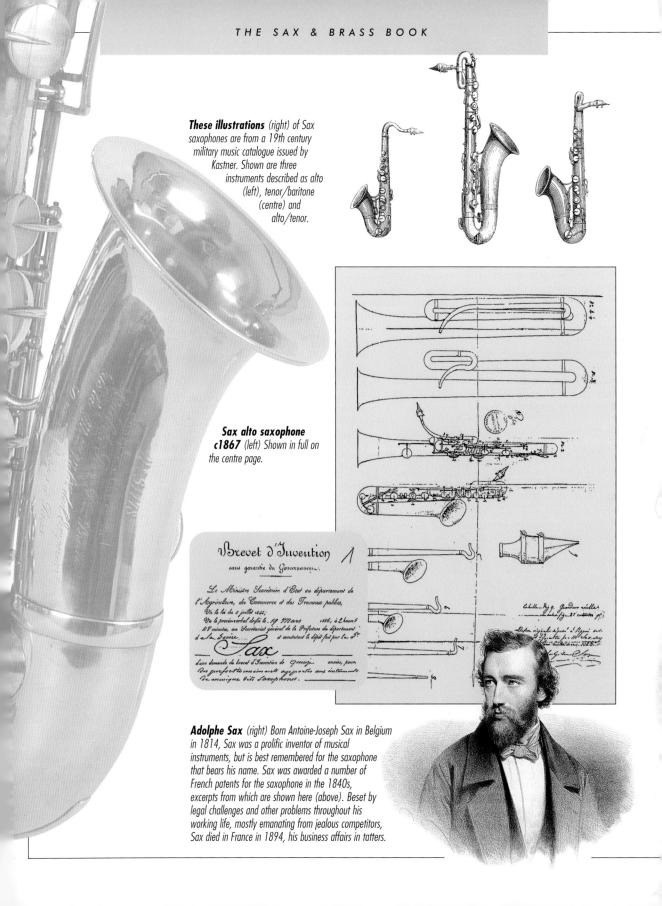

These illustrations (right) of Sax saxophones are from a 19th century military music catalogue issued by Kastner. Shown are three instruments described as alto (left), tenor/baritone (centre) and alto/tenor.

Sax alto saxophone c1867 (left) Shown in full on the centre page.

Adolphe Sax (right) Born Antoine-Joseph Sax in Belgium in 1814, Sax was a prolific inventor of musical instruments, but is best remembered for the saxophone that bears his name. Sax was awarded a number of French patents for the saxophone in the 1840s, excerpts from which are shown here (above). Beset by legal challenges and other problems throughout his working life, mostly emanating from jealous competitors, Sax died in France in 1894, his business affairs in tatters.

Sax tenor saxophone c1866
(right) A slightly earlier example than
the baritone on the opposite page, this
is another piece of 19th century
handiwork from the Sax factory in
France. In the mid 1840s, soon after
Sax had first demonstrated his new
saxophone, the Belgian-born instrument
maker had enjoyed what seemed on
the face of it to be a piece of
remarkable good fortune. The French
government held a public contest to
decide which maker's instruments
should be used in the military bands of
the time — and Sax won. However, this
prompted a steady stream of legal and
other attacks on Sax and his factory.
French instrument makers were horrified
at the success of this upstart foreigner,
and Adolphe Sax was dogged by a
series of court battles and regular
vilification for the rest of his life.

This group of instruments shows
the relative sizes, to scale, of the four
most popular types of saxophone.

baritone   tenor   alto   soprano

32

Selmer Made
ADOLPHE TENOR SAX

for

£24 NET PRO.
(PERMGOLD FINISH)

This instrument is the only possible
reconciliation between a first-class
discrimination and a second-class
pocket. It looks as good as the top-
priced instruments, sounds as well,
is guaranteed as long, and lacks for
nothing in the way of modern
improvements. Since it is made by
SELMER, it is an instrument for
ambitious players with shrewd
judgment.
Apply it to whatever test you like,
buy it and then choose a Clarinet
with the money you save.

Alto - - - £21.0.0

Baritone - - £31.10.0
(All Instruments complete with fine quality case
and accessories).

Or on the Trade's Most
Favourable Hire Purchase
Terms for a few shillings
a week.

SELMER

Davis Building, 12 Moor St., London, W.1
Phones : Gerrard 2575/6

This 1933 ad (above) from the
British musicians' magazine Melody
Maker shows how the French company

Selmer used the "Adolphe" name after
they bought the Sax company from
Adolphe Sax's sons in the early 1920s.

When Adolphe Sax *began his saxophone experiments, 19th century makers still built all brass instruments with traditional "cup" mouthpieces.*

Sax baritone saxophone c1876 *(left) This is one of a family of saxophones that the instrument's inventor, the Belgian-born Adolphe Sax, built in France during the last half of the 19th century. Joining his father Charles-Joseph Sax's firm of brass instrument builders during the late 1820s, while still in his teens, Sax at first interested himself by examining the existing clarinet and working on some modifications and "improvements". The young Adolphe Sax soon developed his own bass clarinet. In the early 1840s, having decided to move from Belgium to Paris, France, Sax set his heart on developing "families" of new instruments. At first he came up with a set of matched valved bugles (or "saxhorns"), but soon a more interesting instrument evolved. Sax probably combined the single-reed mouthpiece of his bass clarinet with an ophicleide, a bass brass instrument of the keyed-bugle family that had been around since the 1820s. With further modifications, Sax came up with his saxophone, first demonstrated around 1842, a brand new instrument that waited 80 years to find real popularity.*

This Sax baritone *of the 1870s (left) is typical of early saxophones in its key placements and the relatively narrow dimensions of the body.*

This close-up *(above) of a Sax alto saxophone of the 1860s shows the information that Adolphe had engraved on most of his instruments. He'd moved to Paris in 1841, with a shop in Rue St. Georges.*

The distinctive shape of the saxophone has not changed significantly throughout its history. Although it is made of brass, it is classified as a woodwind instrument because its basic sound is created by a clarinet-type mouthpiece (above) and a wooden reed. The mouthpiece has a slot cut into the underside, which is very slightly curved. A single, flat reed is clamped against this and vibrates when blown. The gap between the reed and the curved surface is called the 'lay'. There are innumerable combinations of lay, of internal dimensions and of reed strength. Players gradually work out the combination which suits them. Like all woodwind instruments, the saxophone is essentially a pipe with holes in it. These holes are covered and uncovered by an elaborate system of padded keys, operated by springs, rods and levers.

Sax instruments 1860s (above)
This engraving, which first appeared in Le Monde Illustré during November 1864, demonstrates the range of instruments being produced at the Sax workshops of the period and shown at a contemporary exhibition.

Sax soprano saxophone c1862
(above) The soprano saxophone might have seemed like a metal clarinet to Sax, who had already produced instruments of the clarinet family before inventing the saxophone. The straight body of the soprano has a bad effect on its tuning stability, and this has caused problems for makers through the years.

C-Melody Saxophone The most popular saxophone among amateur players in the jazz-crazy 1920s, the C-melody barely outlived the decade (1924 King ad, below). It was very user-friendly for a beginner, because it

could be played with piano direct from the song copy, without complicated transposition. As a solo instrument the C-melody was fine, but there was no place for it in the evolving saxophone section. Old C-melodys continued as

beginners' instruments for many years, and unscrupulous dealers would sometimes pass them off as tenors. Gradually, however, their numbers declined and it is now rare to find one in playable condition. Although he always denied the fact, Coleman Hawkins began his professional career on C-melody. There is a photo of him playing one, as a very young man with Mamie Smith's Original Jazz Hounds, to prove it. The greatest exponent of the instrument, however, was Frankie Trumbauer (above, third from left, playing alto in Paul Whiteman's section). Trumbauer (1901-1956) was a virtuoso whose technique was the envy of all other saxophonists. Even the legendary Benny Carter, the most accomplished and polished of players, confessed, "I never had his facility." Not only did Trumbauer master all the conventional techniques, he perfected a number of 'freak' styles, such as double and triple tongueing (now obsolete). The record of his spectacular showpiece number, 'Trumbology', was in every saxophonist's collection. His opening solo on 'Singing The Blues', with Bix Beiderbecke, is still often played note-for-note today.

Conn C-Melody saxophone c1922

Be With You One Hour Tonight', and Hawkins's full, sensuous tone and great, looping phrases were if anything even more impressive than what he'd done on 'Hello Lola'. Hawkins found a voice for the tenor saxophone, a voice that commanded respect and attention. For almost a decade he was acknowledged as the first and greatest saxophonist in the world, and everyone copied him. He had no rivals, only followers. He became known by two nicknames: Hawk, for obvious reasons, and Bean. No one knew how he came by this curious appellation, although Hawkins believed that it was "because the shape of my head resembled a haricot bean".

In 1934, bored with Henderson's band, Hawk came to Britain to play as a star guest with Jack Hylton's show-band. So ecstatic was his reception, especially among other musicians, that he remained in Europe for five years and had an incalculable effect on the development of European jazz.

HAWK'S BODY AND SOUL

In 1939, almost as soon as he had returned to the US, Hawk recorded the version of 'Body And Soul' which is generally agreed to be his masterpiece. It was also a hugely popular hit, a fact which surprised Hawkins as much as anyone. The piece had been a last-minute addition to the session and the melody of the well-known ballad is scarcely recognisable beneath the luxuriant foliage of his invention.

Hawkins talked in 1956 about the recording of 'Body And Soul': "I didn't even bother to listen to it afterwards. Got through playing it, packed my horn up and walked out." A few weeks later he heard it on the radio as he sat drinking in a bar. "A girl sitting there said, 'Is that your record?' I listened and said, 'That's my tone, more or less.' I said, 'That's funny.' This thing actually sounded good. I was surprised. That was the best number of the date – the one I thought was nothing." In that same 1956 interview Hawk recalled that at first other musicians began telling him he'd played "wrong notes" on the tune: their way of objecting to how he'd implied extra chords. "Of course, that's extremely common now," he said. "It certainly wasn't common before I did 'Body And Soul', I can tell you that."

Every budding saxophonist – among them such future saxophone giants as Sonny Rollins and John Coltrane – bought the transcribed sheet music of Hawkins's solo and struggled through it in the hope that something would rub off.

Almost until the end of his life in the late 1960s Hawkins remained a tough, combative musician, on the lookout for new ideas and challenges. The boy whose career began with Mamie Smith's Jazz Hounds was playing alongside Thelonious Monk in his late fifties, and giving his juniors a run for their money.

Among Hawkins' most distinguished adherents was Leon "Chu" Berry (1910-41). While Hawk was away in Europe, Chu became the style leader at home. Berry's style was more fulsome and his tone rather sweeter, but nonetheless he was clearly a Hawkins man. In 1939 he joined Cab Calloway's hugely successful orchestra as tenor saxophone soloist and "straw boss" (deputy leader), becoming largely responsible for the superbly clean and well-defined sound of Calloway's saxophone section. He was killed in a road accident in 1941 at the age of just 31.

Ben Webster (1909-73) yielded to no one in his admiration for Hawkins, but his own style grew in a different direction. In 1939 he joined Duke Ellington and his famous orchestra, the first featured tenor saxophone soloist that Duke ever had, and his tough/tender, gruff/melting sound became one of its great glories during the early 1940s. 'Just A Sittin And A Rockin' and 'Cottontail' were his most celebrated numbers with the band, the first silky and insinuating, the second urgent and driving.

Later, Webster went on to develop a breathy, blowsy style of playing ballads which had only been hinted at in his Ellington days. Toward the end of his life in the 1970s Webster moved to Europe where he was treated as a hero and a great artist. In his later work the sound of breath gradually invades the notes, each phrase ending with a vibrating column of air and slowly fading into silence, like the Cheshire Cat's grin.

Hawk's equivalent on the alto saxophone was Benny Carter (1907-). Where Hawkins was forceful and commanding, Carter played with a bright and debonair manner. His sound had a kind of fluffy lightness about it, and his improvised lines seemed to sing. Carter also came to work in Europe during the late 1930s, principally as guest arranger with Henry Hall's BBC Dance Orchestra, and his influence was felt almost as strongly as that of Hawkins.

Carter was a prodigy. Not only was he the finest alto saxophonist of his day, he also played the trumpet better than most trumpeters. And at the slightest excuse he would take solos on all the other saxophones, on piano and on clarinet, and also oblige with the occasional song. The word used then and ever afterwards to describe Carter's playing was elegant. Carter's elegance, poise, self-assurance and the creamy, unruffled surface of his sound have not always been in favour with critics of grittier tastes, but these qualities captivated musicians. His European recordings, especially those in Paris with Coleman Hawkins and Django Reinhardt, are among the best he ever made. On returning to the US he led his own big band and from the 1950s he lived in southern California, enjoying a comfortable career as a composer of film and television music – and playing as well as ever. In August 1997 Benny Carter reached the age of 90, and he was still playing very well indeed.

Unlike Hawkins, Benny Carter had a rival: Johnny Hodges (1907-70), alto saxophone star of Duke Ellington's orchestra. Hodges played with two basic voices: a cryptic, swinging style composed of short, punchy phrases; and a swooningly romantic one, characterised by swoops and slides (called glissandi in the trade), so smooth that you could scarcely believe he was playing an instrument with keys on it at all. For 35 years – with occasional interruptions – the unique sound of Hodges dominated the Ellington orchestra, either leading the saxophone section or playing solo, whether on melting, romantic pieces like 'Warm Valley' or on bright, springy numbers such as 'Junior Hop'.

Hodges was also one of the very few players of his generation to play the soprano; in fact it was his first instrument. He hailed originally from New England at a time when in that part of America very few musicians, black or white, had much idea about jazz. As a teenager Hodges had taken lessons from Sidney Bechet, and this early contact obviously had a lasting effect.

Hodges absorbed a great deal at an impressionable age from the great New Orleans master, learning about the blues and about the rhythmic element known as swing which was, essentially, a New Orleans invention. Hodges took up the alto and joined Ellington at the age of 21 – and was still a member when he died 42 years later.

Hodges recorded on soprano quite a bit during his early career with Ellington, using it particularly in blues numbers such as 'That's The Blues Old Man', but he put it aside in 1940

– reportedly because Ellington refused to pay him extra for playing two instruments – and never touched it again. Hodges had a very basic attitude towards money: he insisted on being paid in cash after every performance, on the grounds that he refused to owe money to anyone or have any owed to him.

From the beginning, alto and tenor have been the most commonly used saxophones, although the baritone made quite early appearances, usually as a "double" for the alto. Nevertheless, almost up until the 1950s if you'd asked a moderately keen jazz fan to name two baritone players they would have got stuck after naming just one. There was simply no one of comparable stature to Duke Ellington's Harry Carney (1910-74). He was the band's longest-serving member, with 47 years' unbroken service, and as Duke's friend and confidant was the rock upon which his sound was built.

Carney's vast, resonant tone coloured the entire band, and when he played occasional solos the effect was rather like Paul Robeson's voice: dignified and statuesque. The only other baritone player of note during the swing era was Count Basie's Jack Washington, who played excellent occasional solos with a slightly lighter touch than Carney, but who attracted little attention from fans or critics.

The baritone saxophone became more common as a jazz instrument when the saxophone section of the American dance orchestra expanded from four to five during the late 1930s and early 1940s. There were simply more baritone players around, and more baritones for them to play. This was not the case with the less favoured members of the saxophone family, most of which virtually disappeared from view.

FRANKIE AND THE C-MELODIES

The C-melody saxophone had a great start in the jazz world, being featured on a number of Bix Beiderbecke's classic recordings, notably 'Singing The Blues'. The player was Frankie Trumbauer (1901-56) whose light, cool sound and witty lines make him one of the most attractive jazz saxophonists of the 1920s.

Technically the C-melody is a slightly smaller version of the tenor and pitched a tone higher in the key of C – hence the name. All the other saxophones are "transposing" instruments, which means that their "open" scale – equivalent to the white notes on the piano – is not C but B-flat or E-flat. The same is

Coleman Hawkins was living and working in Europe, between 1934 and 1939, when a dispute arose between the US and British musicians' unions which forbade American musicians from playing public engagements in the UK. Hawkins' agent got around this problem by advertising his appearances as 'Demonstrating Selmer Saxophones'. His loyalty to Selmer was total, and the company supplied him with instruments throughout his subsequent career.

Hawkins had his tenor triple gold-plated, claiming it enhanced the tone. Other musicians wondered how he supported its immense weight for hours on end, but he appeared not to notice. His use of the Otto Link metal mouthpiece helped make it popular. By the 1950s, most jazz players used metal, but many still preferred Ebonite or even plastic. Metal (stainless steel or bronze) gives a harder sound, but tone depends ultimately on the player.

38

Coleman Hawkins (above in the late 1940s with a young, moustached Miles Davis) was a forceful individual. Until old age and indifference overtook him, he dressed in style, drove expensive cars and ate and drank the very best. His long stay in Europe (above right with Dutch band the Ramblers) gave him an air of sophistication that intimidated many of his colleagues. At the same time, he could be remarkably tight-fisted. Cornettist Rex Stewart, who knew him well, once remarked: 'Hawk wouldn't part with a dime to see the Statue of Liberty doing a striptease on the Brooklyn Bridge at high noon.' His self-confidence, almost as much as his musical genius, led Hawkins to welcome the bebop revolution of the mid-1940s. He embraced it as a challenge rather than seeing it as a threat. Miles Davis, Thelonious Monk, Allen Eager, Max Roach and others benefited from his patronage.

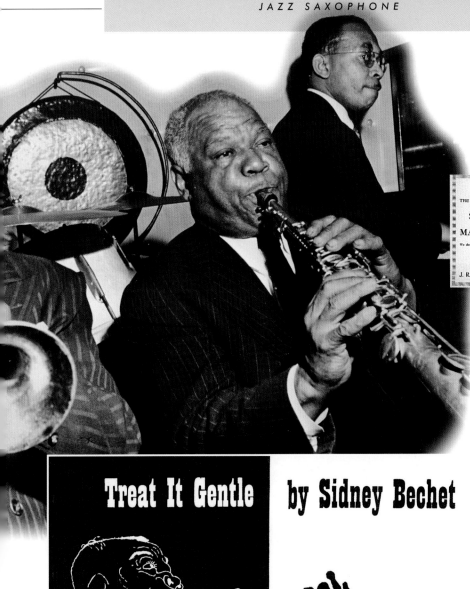

Sidney Bechet (left, with trumpeter Oran 'Hot Lips' Page, drummer Freddie Moore and pianist Lloyd Phillips in the late 1940s) was the first virtuoso of the soprano saxophone. In 1919, on

LAFLEUR

THE HOUSE USED BY ALL PROFESSIONALS OF STANDING

Only Official London Representatives of

SELMER (Paris) SAXOPHONES
& WOOD WIND INSTRUMENTS
AND

MARTIN (Elkhart) SAXOPHONES
& BRASS INSTRUMENTS

We do not give Instruments away for advertisement, our productions sell on their merits

J. R. LAFLEUR & SON LTD., 147, Wardour Street, London, W.1

his first trip abroad with the Southern Syncopated Orchestra, Bechet saw an early-model soprano sax in London's Lafleur store. He was attracted by the look of the instrument and bought it on the spot. Almost immediately, it replaced the clarinet as his main instrument. His sweeping tone and wide vibrato expressed his personality to perfection. To enhance this effect, he had the lay of his mouthpiece enlarged several times, until it was so open that no-one else could ever have played it. Towards the end of his life, when he had become a superstar in France, his adopted homeland, Bechet rarely improvised his solos. Like Louis Armstrong at the same stage, he had arrived at variations on his favourite tunes that pleased him and saw no reason to change them. During this period Bechet also composed several orchestral pieces, the best known being the ballet 'La Nuit est une Sorcière', an intensely dramatic work in the late-Romantic style. As a New Orleans creole, Bechet had always considered himself to be a sort of Frenchman, and in his final decade he became more and more French. His tone and vibrato grew to sound uncannily like those of the great chanteuse Edith Piaf. He also adopted the Gallic custom of keeping two households, presided over by his wife and his mistress respectively, on opposite sides of Paris. It was not until after Bechet's death in 1959 that the soprano saxophone became a commonly used jazz instrument.

Treat It Gentle **by Sidney Bechet**

The Jazz Book Club
Cassell · London 1962

true of the trumpet, the flugelhorn and most other valved brass instruments, and also the clarinet. This is confusing enough to the lay person, but the confusion is made worse by the practice of treating the open key as C, regardless of the fact that it isn't. So C on the alto saxophone is actually E-flat, and C on the tenor is actually B-flat. This affects all the other notes in turn, so an F on the piano is D on the alto and G on the tenor, and so on. I trust you are now thoroughly confused.

The C-melody saxophone had been designed to be free of these entanglements. You could pick it up and play the notes off a song sheet along with a pianist and you would both be playing in the same key. During the saxophone craze of the 1920s the C-melody was the big favourite with amateur players for this very reason. But it didn't fit into saxophone sections, which had overlapping ranges of B-flat and E-flat instruments, and the C-melody virtually expired with its decade. However, here is an item of late news: the British saxophonist and composer John Dankworth recently took up the C-melody saxophone and now regularly features it with his Dankworth Generation Band, the outfit which he co-leads with his son, bassist Alec Dankworth.

THE BOTTOM END

The bass saxophone was always something of a problem. To begin with, it was heavy and bulky and a pain to carry about. More to the point, it didn't have a clear-cut role. It could be used in the rhythm section as a substitute for the string bass or tuba or as part of the Dixieland ensemble – sometimes a bit of both. In the wrong hands it was a terrible liability, because if the notes weren't punched out cleanly it just blundered about, getting in everybody's way.

The undoubted master of the bass saxophone was Adrian Rollini (1904-56) whose crisp, decisive attack can be heard on many records from the 1920s, especially those of Red Nichols & His Five Pennies. Benny Goodman included a bass saxophone in his sax section for a while in the early 1940s. Britain's leading bass saxophonist Harry Gold (1907-) celebrated his 90th birthday with a huge jazz party at which he played the enormous instrument for several hours with no apparent ill effects.

There is one other essential name in the first half of the jazz saxophone story, and that is Lester Young (1909-59). He did the

unthinkable by daring to play the tenor as though Coleman Hawkins had never existed. His tone was light and his phrasing springy. Where Hawkins had a tendency to plough doggedly up and down every possible chord that he could fit into a tune – and he had a wonderful ear which allowed him to alter and elaborate the harmonies of a tune endlessly – Young, on the other hand, would dance lightly over them.

There were many who simply refused to take Young seriously at first. But by about 1938, when Count Basie's band had become established with Young as its star soloist, it was clear that there were now in existence two distinct and separate approaches to the jazz tenor saxophone. And that's the way it has been ever since. Young's playing had a profound effect on players of the next generation.

Young also introduced a new technical trick, producing the same note at different densities by using different fingerings. This is possible only on certain notes, and must be used sparingly. Most commonly it's used around the break between the first and second octave. The correct fingering for middle D, for instance, is to have all the main keys closed and the octave key engaged. But it is possible to play with the octave disengaged and all the keys, including the high D, open. By alternating the two you can produce the same note sounding like "mm-ah-mm-ah". By slipping from closed to open in one movement, at the same time increasing the volume, it is possible, with practice, for the skilled saxophonist to make a sound something like "Wa!"

While we are on the subject of tonal effects, Ben Webster used to produce a kind of yodel on certain notes. One of these was F in the second register, which he managed by fingering F normally, at the same time holding open the high-F key and making a big vibrato. It is best to practice these effects well away from any form of human or animal habitation.

Now that we have met the pioneers and the main members of the saxophone family this may be a good moment to pause and consider the saxophone itself – as a piece of machinery, as a musical instrument and as a jazz icon. It was invented by the Belgian musical instrument maker Adolphe Sax in the 1840s, long before jazz ever existed.

Although it is made of brass the saxophone is really a woodwind instrument, with a clarinet-type mouthpiece and reed, and with fingering similar to that of the oboe. It was only one of many new instruments to emerge around the middle of the 19th century. Precision engineering made huge advances at the time, making possible all kinds of musical innovations. Some of these proved useful and have lasted, like the modern systems of keys and valves, while other instruments such as the ophicleide, the surrusophone and the phono-fiddle look today like the work of some genial lunatic.

Adolphe Sax originally developed the saxophone for use in military bands and at the time of his death in 1894 that's where it seemed to be stuck. There are few sounds less beguiling than that of a saxophone blown lustily in the open air, and no one predicted much of a future for the instrument. It was the popularity of ragtime music and the craze for public dancing after World War I that brought the saxophone indoors, which is where it met jazz.

The American dance orchestra as it evolved in the 1920s made great use of saxophones. Two or three of them playing together made more noise than a dozen violins, while the syrupy, quavering tone adopted by early players sounded so offensive to the refined ear that the saxophone soon came to symbolise the avant-garde, the horrors of the modern world or even The End Of Civilisation As We Know It. Naturally this made it a great favourite with the younger generation, who were also attracted to its disreputable American upbringing. In the first quarter of this century it was quite common to find vaudeville acts featuring as "novelty" instruments the whole family of saxophones, from the tiny sopranino to the mighty bass or even the gargantuan contra-bass. These acts leaned heavily towards popping sounds produced by "slap-tonguing", as well as barnyard noises and similar effects.

If in the mid 1920s a young man of respectable background owned a saxophone and claimed to be learning to play it, this was universally understood as a gesture of mild revolt – rather like growing one's hair long in the 1960s or wearing corduroy trousers in the 1930s. In the eager hands of an army of such rebels the instrument gave rise to the famous old joke about the definition of a gentleman being someone who owns a saxophone... but refrains from playing it. The joke was later transferred to the banjo.

Saxophones, mainly alto and C-melody types, sold in their hundreds of thousands. A typical British ad, by Keith Prowse of Bond Street in London, appeared in the Christmas 1925 issue of *Sound Wave* magazine and offered saxophones from £20 ($32), banjos from 48/- (£2.40, about $3.80) as well as something that the supplier called a "Jazz Set" for 27/6 (£1.37, about $2.20) along with a miscellany of mouth-organs, musical saws, Jew's harps and toy bagpipes.

OPERATION SAXOPHONE

The clear implication of all this is that back in the 1920s the saxophone was not marketed as a proper musical instrument at all, but as a rather expensive toy. The musical world also failed to acknowledge the saxophone. On the rare occasions when a saxophone was required to be added to a symphony orchestra – almost always for works by French composers such as Bizet, Delibes, Saint-Saens and Ravel – the person brought in to play it was referred to not as a saxophonist or even a player but as a "saxophone operator". Apart from the Paris Conservatoire it seemed that no musical academy was willing even to recognise the instrument's existence. When British jazzman John Dankworth was a student at the Royal Academy Of Music in London back in the mid 1940s he found it best to keep secret the fact that he even owned a saxophone, let alone that he played it in public.

Like most forms of art, jazz is at its best when important and respectable people want nothing to do with it. The saxophone developed into the marvellously flexible and expressive instrument it is today precisely because proper musicians would not touch it. It was not usually taught in music colleges, there was virtually no "serious" music written for it, and finding methodical instruction manuals was virtually impossible. As a result there was no correct way to play the saxophone and no correct sound to aim at. The only official classical sound was the one developed at the Paris Conservatoire, presumably because at first the instrument had a role in French military music. (This in fact was the role for which Sax had invented it in the first place.)

Picture the United States in the 1920s. It had a much smaller and more scattered population than today, radio was in its infancy and confined to local stations of limited range, and live popular entertainment was provided by dance halls, vaudeville theatres and speakeasies in the towns and cities and all manner of travelling shows in other parts. In such circumstances musicians learned from one another and,

Buescher was one of the most popular brands of saxophone in the US, especially during the 1920s boom in the instrument's popularity. The company had been founded in 1888 by Gus Buescher. He had recently left the Conn company in Elkhart, Indiana, the town that soon became the wind musical instrument capital of America. Buescher set up his own firm and concentrated at first on trumpets. These stylish ads (above) date from the mid 1940s, when Buescher were pushing their new 400 saxophone model.

This ad (above) from the American jazz magazine Metronome in 1946 might well have different implications for the modern reader, but the moody saxophonist here looks to be high on the entirely legal sonic potential of his brand new Buescher 400 axe.

42

Rudy Vallee (left) was an early pop idol, whose high voice, crooning 'Vagabond Lover', prompted scenes of mass hysteria in the 1920s. To get started in showbusiness he taught himself the alto saxophone, the fashionable instrument to play at the time. He was only ever a moderate player. Vallee was the first singer to use a microphone, amplifier and speakers in live performance.

Buescher 400 tenor saxophone c1943 (left) Buescher, like their chief rivals Conn as well as Martin, made their instruments in Elkhart, Indiana. No doubt spies would slip into one another's factories on a regular basis. Thus the features and designs of the instruments of these three companies are often similar. However, Buescher's unique touch on their 400 saxophone, introduced around 1942, was the relatively large flare of the bell, requiring a supportive metal strip underneath and delivering a suitably bigger sound than many other saxes.

The keys for the left hand (see detail inset here) on many American instruments continued into the 1940s to use what would today be considered an old-fashioned layout, whereby the player must move the left-hand little finger awkwardly across the keys. Selmer's Balanced Action model of the early 1930s had introduced a more player-friendly "circular" arrangement of these same keys, but the French influence took a while to reach the US makers. As can be seen in the photograph, Buescher also used this key cluster to show off the model number of their 400 saxophone.

Buescher 400 alto saxophone c1945 (left) The 400 alto saxophone shared the novel large bell flare of the tenor variety, and the Buescher company's 400 models were also unusual in that they were without the guards used by most makers to protect the bottom B and Bb keys. Instead, Buescher decided that they would move the relevant toneholes around the back of the bell, theoretically out of harm's way. Buescher's other main sax model of the time was the Aristocrat. The company was eventually sold to Selmer in 1963, but instruments made after this are generally not well regarded.

Buescher invariably used this logo (above) on the saxophones produced during this period. The interlinked characters recall contemporary US automobile logos that were designed as one continuous strip of metal.

Johnny Hodges (above, with Duke Ellington) was a vital member of the Ellington orchestra. His thick, warm alto tone imparted a glow to the saxophone section for more than 40 years. The section itself sounded like no other, a collection of individual voices rather than a highly drilled ensemble. In 1933 (top) it consisted of (left to right) Otto Hardwicke, Harry Carney, Barney Bigard and Hodges. The four later became five, with the addition of Ben Webster's tenor in 1939.

43

because their circle of acquaintance was limited, they tended to develop recognisable local styles. The saxophone, having no orthodoxy to begin with, was very sensitive to this process.

A typical product is the style known as "Texas tenor", beefy-toned and loaded with blues inflections. The family resemblance is quite evident in the playing of musicians like Buddy Tate (1915-), Arnett Cobb (1918-89) and Herschel Evans (1909-39), all Texans and born within the space of nine years, even though each has his own distinct musical voice. When music is learned by ear, like speech it develops an accent.

J IS FOR JAZZ

It is often said that the saxophone resembles the human voice, and this is true. The sound of the voice expresses the thoughts, moods and personality of its owner. It unwittingly betrays our age and even our state of health, and no two human voices are exactly alike. The same applies to the saxophone. Think of Coleman Hawkins and Lester Young. If you knew nothing whatever about them you would still be able to make a pretty good guess at their respective personalities simply by hearing them play. One is forceful, abrasive and unsentimental; the other dreamy, whimsical and shy. What is it about the saxophone that gives it this chameleon-like character?

To begin with, it is a theoretically imperfect instrument. Unlike the clarinet, which is cylindrical, the saxophone is a cone. For reasons too boring and complicated to go into here this makes the fingering easier but at the same time makes it more difficult to play in tune. Because the development of orchestral instruments over the past 200 years has been largely a laborious quest for perfect intonation, this is a disadvantage. On the other hand, the cone shape makes it easier to bend notes up or down and also facilitates the production of funny noises (as the aforementioned novelty groups discovered).

In fact the saxophone doesn't really have much of a "core" sound. It merely responds to the way you blow it. This is what makes living close to a saxophone beginner such a character-building experience. However, once a budding player learns to control the instrument reasonably well this apparent limitation turns out to be a most precious quality. It means that you can imagine the sound you want to make and, with time, practice and a modicum of talent, it will emerge.

That must have been what Hawkins did back in the 1920s,

except that he had to do his imagining from scratch. Since those same 1920s the saxophone has symbolised jazz. Its appearance was distinctive and quite unlike that of any traditional musical instrument, and most saxophones were even helpfully shaped like the letter J for Jazz.

In the years following World War I there was a fashion in Bohemian circles for Negro art, which included some early attempts to colonise jazz and the blues in the interests of the artistic avant-garde. As usually happens, the innovations of a minority became gradually diluted into a widely held collection of popular notions and fashionable beliefs. Among these was the idea that we were all over-civilised and needed to shed our inhibitions (Freud had got mixed up in it somewhere). The way to do this was to kick over the traces, to shock respectable society by staying up all night, and to cultivate an air of decadence – whatever that might be. Vital elements seemed to be dancing and making a lot of noise. Dancing meant jazz. Jazz meant saxophones and black people.

It is a well established fact that there is nothing young people like better than jumping about to loud noises, and as a justification for having a jolly time this was as good as any other. But viewed from outside and from different ideologies it all looked far from harmless.

When the Nazis came to power in Germany they saw it like this: fashionable American decadence is a weapon devised by the international Jewish conspiracy to undermine German youth; it seduces them with the degraded music of inferior races played on barbarous instruments. There is a famous Nazi propaganda poster warning of the dangers of entartete Musik (degenerate music). It depicts a figure half-monkey, half-black man (standing for racial impurity), dressed in a top hat (for international capitalism) and a Star of David (for Jew), blowing a stylised saxophone (for decadence).

In the Soviet Union the party line swung back and forth. For a while it maintained that jazz was the musical expression of an oppressed race and therefore to be encouraged, but in 1949 it came down firmly with the view that the whole thing was bourgeois-imperialist propaganda and had no place in the Workers' State. Once jazz was abolished there was no need for saxophones, so the saxophone players in all the state bands were ordered to hand in their instruments. Since under Socialism there could be no such thing as unemployment these musicians were then re-registered as clarinetists or flautists or bassoonists, regardless of whether they could play those instruments or not. That is one of the saxophone's many excellent virtues: it upsets the kind of people who deserve to be upset, and makes them look ridiculous.

Before we leave the swing era – roughly 1935 to 1945 – let's take a look at something that was developed and brought to a peak of perfection by the big-bands of that period, namely the saxophone section. When you consider the matter, there are very few basic orchestral formats in Western music. There is the symphony orchestra (strings, woodwind, brass, percussion), there's the military band (woodwind, brass and percussion), the brass band... and what else?

The only obvious example that comes to mind is the jazz big-band (saxes, brass and rhythm). Wynton Marsalis calls this "the American orchestra", which is a good name because it is an American invention. It grew out of the American dance orchestra of the 1920s, it is powered by a jazz rhythm section and it features a section or "choir" of saxophones.

As it finally settled down in the late 1930s the saxophone section consisted of two altos, two tenors and baritone, and this is still the usual big-band format. Earlier line-ups included two altos and tenor, and two altos and two tenors. This last combination remained popular for many years and can be heard on all Benny Goodman's early hits. Later variations included alto, three tenors and baritone (Woody Herman 1947-9), and soprano, two altos, two tenors and baritone (the Thad Jones-Mel Lewis Band of the late 1960s and early 1970s). The bass saxophone also made occasional appearances, notably with Goodman (1942-3).

You need a little historical imagination now to understand what a revolutionary sound the saxophone section was, not only because the instruments sounded different from previous ones but because of the way in which they were harmonised. The most common way of combining the four or five saxophones was in "close harmony", where they would all move in a tightly-knit formation rather like a flock of birds wheeling. This, too, was a uniquely American sound, and one that had probably derived from the barbershop vocal style and the tradition of black spiritual choirs.

The saxophone section offered a warm, sentimental, enfolding sound which some found irresistibly glamorous and attractive. Others hated it with a deep loathing for being mawkish, syrupy and maudlin. Glenn Miller added another spoonful of sugar to the confection when he put a clarinet on top of one alto, two tenors and baritone to create his theme-tune, 'Moonlight Serenade'.

CHASIN' THE BIRD

Lester Young had broken the taboo on light-toned tenor saxophones and established a new approach to the instrument. In the same way a few years later Charlie Parker (1920-55) would break the taboo on heavy-toned altos. By leading the bebop revolution that took place during the 1940s Parker changed a lot of other things, too. But purely as an instrumentalist his influence was profound.

The previous models for alto saxophonists had been Benny Carter and Johnny Hodges, born respectively in New York City and Cambridge, Massachusetts. Parker came from Kansas City, the northern apex of a great triangle whose southern base-points lie in Texas to the west and Georgia to the east. Within this triangle flourished the blues in all its myriad varieties. To all black musicians brought up there – and some white players too – the blues was a native language and its accents flavoured every note they played, sang, or even spoke.

When the veteran saxophonist Garvin Bushell travelled through Kansas City and the south-west in the 1920s he noticed that "most bands included a saxophone. They just played the blues, one after another, in different tempos". Because of the saxophone's chameleon-like ability to reproduce the sounds that players imagine in their heads, virtually all saxophonists raised in the blues triangle played with a blues tone and inflection. This is where Parker's thick, full, thoroughly indelicate tone had its origins. The sound is unmistakable, like the sound of Armstrong's trumpet. It has none of the elegance of Benny Carter or the sensuousness of Johnny Hodges. The tone is brusque, with a curious, thick-tongued articulation, rather like a lisp.

At first hearing, Parker can seem incomprehensible, his solos a wild, illogical jumble. At least that's how it seemed to a lot of people in the 1940s when his early records began to appear. Now, half a century later, that first shock may have passed. But there's still nothing in the least bit cosy about Charlie Parker or the music he pioneered, which went under

45

46

Conn "Big Bore" tenor saxophone c1930 (left) Conn was among the leading US manufacturers of saxophones during the fad for the instrument in the 1920s, and had in fact produced the first American-made saxophone back in the 1880s. The company had been established by Charles Gerard Conn in the 1870s in Elkhart, Indiana, which became the base for most of the leading US wind instrument makers. Conn's earliest saxophones were the Wonder models, but later instruments included this "Big Bore" and the Connqueror series.

Lester Young (below) emerged from military detention in 1946 and restarted his career with a recording contract with the new Aladdin label and triumph in the Esquire jazz poll. Lester's strange way of holding the tenor out to one side is caught in a famous action shot (bottom).

Chu Berry (above) was the only tenor saxophonist to offer a serious challenge to Coleman Hawkins in his own, big-toned idiom. Through records like 'Ghost Of A Chance' with Cab Calloway and small-band sessions with Lionel Hampton, his reputation was rising fast when he died in a road accident in 1941. Musicians nicknamed a type of Conn sax after him; Lester Young, for example, played a "Chu Berry" model with Basie in the 1930s.

Conn 22-M Conn-o-Sax c1928 (above) This strange-looking instrument with its ball-shaped bell is a soprano-like saxophone in the key of F that Conn first made in 1928. Conn thought players wanted a more piercing tone, and attempted to provide it with the Conn-o-Sax. But players stayed away, and Conn dropped it during 1929.

Conn "Big Bore" alto saxophone c1924 (right) Never an official Conn designation, "Big Bore" is a nickname used by players for Conn's saxes of this era, and describes the wider dimensions of these instruments compared to earlier models made by Conn and other manufacturers. Conn saxophones with these engraved portraits of women (see close-up here) are known as "Lady Face" models. The Big Bore is a classic piece of 1920s saxophone engineering, designed to sound good in dancehalls, and with the then typical key layout that had the two bell keys on opposite sides.

Conn briefly introduced coloured-lacquer saxophones in 1922, as this ad shows, with its "purple, rose, green, blue or striking black and silver". But the idea did not last long at the time.

Conn 10-M tenor saxophone c1935 (right) Conn used model numbers from the late 1910s, and the 10-M tenor and 6-M alto were mainstays of the line for many years. This model shows Conn following Selmer's influence by placing the bell keys on the same side. Other changes compared to the older "Big Bore" brought the keywork closer together, making the instrument easier to play.

Conn's main business for many years had been the manufacture of musical instruments for marching bands, and this heritage is reflected in the company's logo (left), which features three marching musicians. While the saxophone fad of the 1920s and the later popularity of jazz provided new markets for Conn, band instruments remained at the company's heart.

47

the name of bebop. Bebop was hatched at late-night jam-sessions in New York during the early 1940s by young musicians, many of whom were junior members of black swing bands. They were intent upon creating a style that would exist for its own sake and, although they had to play their music in dives and nightclubs, the pioneer beboppers quite definitely considered themselves to be artists, not mere entertainers.

Bebop solos seemed to pass in a blur of notes, the tunes full of strange, jerky stops and starts and the harmonies sounding sour. But once you got attuned to it, bebop was exciting and stimulating. This was the element in which Parker moved.

Parker himself had a go at defining bebop when pushed by a *Down Beat* interviewer in 1949. "It's just music," he said, accurately enough. "It's trying to play clean and looking for the pretty notes." Pressed further, he reckoned a distinctive feature of bebop was its strong feeling for beat. "The beat in a bop band is with the music, against it, behind it. It pushes it. It helps it. Help is the big thing. It has no continuity of beat, no steady chug-chug. Jazz has, and that's why bop is more flexible."

PLASTIC BOP

Parker – universally known as "Bird" – lived such a chaotic, heroin-addicted life that he was constantly finding himself without cash and in urgent need of drugs. At worst he would pawn his saxophone. In later years he developed a strategy for this involving the use of his "spare" alto, a plastic-body instrument made in England and known as a Grafton Acrylic. He could pawn his regular instrument, a King Super-20, and fall back on the Grafton. No pawnbroker on New York's Second Avenue would advance him anything against a plastic instrument, so he was safe. He can be heard playing it on the famous Massey Hall concert recording of May 15th 1953. At a sale of Bird memorabilia held at Christie's auction house in London in September 1994 the unpawnable Grafton fetched £93,500 (about $150,000). The buyer was the mayor of Kansas City, Parker's home town.

Parker's impact was so overwhelming that for many years there was scarcely an alto saxophonist who could resist echoing his tone and phraseology. So it was that Sonny Stitt (1924-82), Sonny Criss (1927-77) and later Phil Woods (1931-) and Jackie McLean (1932-) all began as virtual Bird clones.

Those that did manage to escape Parker's influence could only do so by heading off smartly in the opposite direction, developing lighter and more floating tones than even Benny Carter's and keeping vibrato to a minimum. Lee Konitz (1927-) and Art Pepper were the first to do this, but the one who eventually became the best-known light-toned alto of all was the even more refined Paul Desmond (1924-77).

Because he composed a tune called 'Take Five' and recorded it with the Dave Brubeck Quartet in 1960, Desmond is one of the few saxophonists whose sound is recognised far beyond the confines of the jazz world. Asked once by a magazine journalist to describe his tone, Desmond replied: "I try to sound like a Dry Martini."

One simple fact about bebop and post-war jazz in general is that it involved more notes, delivered at greater speed and in more complex patterns. The saxophone was able to cope mechanically with this, unlike, say, the trombone which required a player of near-genius simply to make it go that fast. But the demand for speed from a saxophone does cut out the possibility of some other options. The huge, cavernous tone of Ben Webster, for instance, requires space in which to operate.

The whole delightful repertoire of slurs, slides, wheezes and growls which had endeared jazz to listeners around the world in earlier times was ditched in favour of speed and pinpoint accuracy. Not surprisingly, this was the point at which deep generation gaps began to appear among jazz lovers, in particular between the boppers and the followers of New Orleans-style music, whom the former dubbed "mouldy figs". When some 20 years or so later those same slurs, wheezes and other sound effects re-appeared it was in the glum and tuneless context of free jazz – where their old fans were unlikely to seek them out. It was during the 1940s, too, that the influence of Lester Young had a powerful delayed-action effect. Tenor saxophonists who had been born in the 1920s reached their teenage years during the swing era when Coleman Hawkins and Lester Young were the two giants of the instrument.

This was the first generation to grow up with radio as a constant presence in the home, and they were able to hear all the great bands of the day in live broadcasts and on record. Whenever Basie's band appeared, the clear, light tones of Lester Young were unmistakable in numbers such as 'Tickle Toe'.

With America's entry into World War II bands soon found themselves short of experienced players and began to recruit promising youngsters below the age of military service, with many Lester Young disciples among them. So it was that a remarkable school of youthful tenor players arose with a sound and approach modelled on Young. Typical of these were Stan Getz (1927-91) and Zoot Sims (1925-85), both seasoned professionals before they were out of their teens.

This turn of events is illustrated by one poignant coincidence. Lester Young himself had a short and unhappy wartime military career, most of it spent in the Detention Barracks at Fort Gordon, Georgia. The day before he was released in December 1945 a band called Kai's Krazy Kats recorded four numbers in a New York studio... the leading soloist being 18-year-old Stan Getz.

In 1947 Getz and Zoot Sims – together with another tenor player, Herbie Steward, and Serge Chaloff on baritone – were members of bandleader Woody Herman's new outfit. They all featured in a number entitled 'Four Brothers' composed by Jimmy Giuffre. This, one of the most beautifully crafted pieces of jazz orchestration outside the work of Ellington, established the sound of the Getz generation as the dominant tenor sound for more than a decade.

The interesting thing about this whole school of players was the diverse ways in which its members developed once they had absorbed Lester's basic approach. Getz for instance first refined the sound to a ghostly paleness, then gradually added colour and vibrancy until at the time of his death in 1991 it had grown to operatic proportions. Sims, beginning close to the same sound, grew warmer and more direct with the years, revealing a strong vein of gruff romanticism. Another Lester Young follower, Wardell Gray (1921-55), developed an incisive edge to his tone that enabled him to manoeuvre elegantly around the tight harmonic curves of bebop. Gray was well known for his tenor duets with Dexter Gordon (1923-89) which they presented in the form of good-natured gladiatorial contests. The most successful of these was 'The Chase' which they recorded several times.

Gordon went on to great success in future years, but there are still musicians and fans who enjoy speculating and claim that if Gray had lived he would surely have grown to become one of the greatest tenor players in jazz history.

Generally speaking, the larger the instrument the harder it is musically to get it to move quickly. In the case of the baritone

saxophone Harry Carney, its greatest exponent in the swing era, had never even contemplated any such idea. The first bebop baritone player of any note was Leo Parker (1925-62, no relation to Bird) and he solved the matter to his own satisfaction by ignoring the problem of incoherence. If the notes all ran together into a kind of animated gurgle, no one was less concerned than Parker.

It was left to Cecil Payne (1922-), Serge Chaloff (1923-57) and Gerry Mulligan (1927-96), and later Pepper Adams (1930-86) and Ronnie Ross (1933-91), to produce a sound on baritone light enough to move as nimbly as a tenor. In the post-war period it at last became possible to name more than one important jazz baritone saxophonist.

SWING, BOP, PROGRESSIVE OR REVIVALIST?

Until the early post-war years jazz had been a fairly straightforward affair. The latest kind was always the most popular and no one questioned the assumption that the newest kind was the best. "In the latest style" was a simple expression of approval.

The term "jazz" was largely dropped in the late 1930s because it was deemed old-fashioned. It was replaced by a new word, "swing". Then along came bebop which enjoyed a brief popular vogue in the late 1940s but was too complicated to be pop music in the way that Goodman and Basie had been. Bebop musicians tended to see themselves as artists, not entertainers, in any case. Pop music now meant singers, often the vocalists who a few years before had been mere appendages of the famous big-bands: Frank Sinatra, Peggy Lee, Dick Haymes, Doris Day.

Suddenly jazz was no longer straightforward. There was bebop and its variants, there was the last gasp of swing, there were strange new brews like the progressive jazz of Stan Kenton, and there was a completely new phenomenon called revivalism – the rediscovery of jazz from the past, either on old records or performed live by ageing players brought out of retirement. From now on it was no good saying that you liked jazz, you had to specify what kind of jazz. And that is the way it has been ever since, only more so. Today, the word "jazz" is virtually meaningless without further definition.

What did all this mean for the saxophone? In revivalist jazz it had no place at all since saxophones did not figure in the

Famed Baritone Sax Artist HARRY CARNEY
with DUKE ELLINGTON BAND
Plays
CONN 12M
Baritone
Saxophone

Harry Carney (above), the first - and for many years only - star of the baritone saxophone, played and endorsed Conn instruments. The C.G. Conn company, brass instrument manufacturers, produced the first American-made saxophone in 1888.

Grafton Acrylic alto saxophone c1951 (left) was conceived by Italian inventor Ettore Sommaruga during World War II, while interned on the Isle of Man as an enemy alien by the British government. The body of the instrument was made of hardened

Superb!
Grafton
"ACRYLIC"
ALTO SAXOPHONE
★ Portrait of famous Band Leader and M.M. Musician of the year
JOHNNY DANKWORTH

plastic and the brass keys bolted onto this. Metal was in short supply, and the Grafton initially met with success. Britian's leading modern jazz musician, Johnny Dankworth, enhanced the instrument's profile by endorsing it and playing it on all his appearances.

Conn "Underslung" alto saxophone c1939 (above) Many professional saxophonists have called the Conn Underslung (above) the best alto saxophone ever made. This classic instrument, with its distinctive octave key slung beneath the crook, has a reputation for reliablity and tuning, and very many are still in daily use. Charlie Parker played a Conn saxophone in the late 1940s.

Charlie Parker acquired a Grafton in about 1951 and kept it as a spare, using it when his regular instrument was in the pawnshop. He played it on the famous Massey Hall concert, recorded in 1953. In 1994 Parker's Grafton was sold at auction for £93,500 (about $154,000). Few Grafton saxophones were exported from Britain. After an initial surge sales fell off badly and full-scale production ended in the mid-1950s. Graftons are now collectors' items.

The King Super-20 alto saxophone c1947 (left) was made by the H.N. White band instrument company of Elkhart, Indiana. Said to have been the last hand-assembled saxophones, they have been favoured by many leading jazz musicians. Wardell Gray and Roland Kirk played the tenor version, as did Johnny Griffin, the 'Little Giant'. Cannonball Adderley always used a Super-20 alto, as did Parker in his final years (except when it was at the pawnbroker's). He played it on the cover of the live album 'Bird At St Nicks' (left) and appeared in King's advertisements (below). The Super-20 came in two ranges, the standard and the Silversonic, with silver crook and bell. Its semi-underslung octave key makes the Super-20 easily recognisable. Although it has a reputation for needing regular servicing, the King is a robust saxophone with great carrying power. It belongs to the era before saxophonists played directly into microphones.

51

This publicity picture (above), put out by Charlie Parker's agent Billy Shaw in about 1948, shows him posing with a saxophone that has a white plastic Brilhart mouthpiece (the inset album has him blowing his King sax). Parker was reputed to be able to play any saxophone, no matter what its condition, and to be a genius at improvised repair jobs. Since he took very little care of his own instrument, and was constantly losing it, this was just as well. The speed and complexity of Parker's musical thought was matched by the dexterity of his technique. He had complete command of the instrument and the transfer of ideas into notes and phrases was instantaneous. Nevertheless, his casual attitude to the physical details of playing did lead to some spectacular mishaps, such as piercing squeaks from untried reeds.

King Super-20 alto 1940s (below) Seen here in its original road-weary case, and just as Parker would have known his.

original New Orleans form of the music. Traditional jazz fans could get very worked up over this matter. When Humphrey Lyttelton, once Britain's leading revivalist, adopted a more open attitude and included the alto saxophonist Bruce Turner in his band, during a concert New Orleans fanatics unfurled a banner bearing the legend: "Go Home, Dirty Bopper!"

In all other forms of jazz the saxophone was more important than ever. Throughout the 1950s the tenor in particular came increasingly to be regarded as the major voice of contemporary jazz. At the beginning of the decade the Four Brothers' sound was dominant with Getz as the leading figure. His recordings from the 1950s include some performances which seem almost superhuman, from every point of view — technique, sound, swing and sheer brilliance of invention.

The term "cool jazz" was applied to the music of Getz and company but, like all such labels, the more closely you examine it the more meaningless it becomes. Getz himself often played with passionate intensity, while Zoot Sims, Al Cohn (1925-88), Bob Cooper (1925-93) and many others were warm, melodic players. Cool jazz was strongly associated with the West Coast of America where many of its leading exponents would spend the daytime working in the Hollywood recording studios and then play jazz at night in the local clubs.

The most prominent alto saxophonist of the West Coast school was Art Pepper (1925-82). His clear, limpid tone gave the impression that the notes were falling effortlessly out of the instrument, like raindrops. He was influenced first by Benny Carter and later by Charlie Parker, but made a conscious effort to avoid becoming a mere echo of Parker.

Pepper wrote in his autobiography, *Straight Life*: "It used to be there was never a solo written in a stock band arrangement for alto. It was all tenor solos — that was 'jazz saxophone'. Charlie Parker made the alto popular, and I thought, 'Well, that's good. That's good.' I noticed that all the tenor players had switched to alto, and they all sounded just like Charlie Parker. Books came out: Bird's solo on this, Bird's solo on that. They'd copy these things off records and practice by the hour Bird's solos and his licks. Everybody sounded like him with the same ugly sound. Guys I'd heard before who had beautiful tones now, all of a sudden, had ugly tones like Bird. Out of tune. Squalling. Squawking. I didn't want to play that way at all, but I realised I had to upgrade my playing and I had to really learn chords and scales. So I didn't copy anyone. I didn't practice much, but I went out and blew and blew and blew. Then I rejoined [Stan] Kenton, and I sounded only like me."

Pepper's reputation rests on a series of records made on the West Coast during the 1950s with a variety of accompaniments ranging from rhythm section to an 11-piece band. There are fewer of these records than there might have been because Pepper served several extended prison terms for drugs offences, the longest being from 1961 to 1964. Curiously enough these protracted lay-offs seem to have had no adverse effect on either his sound or his considerable technique.

SAXOPHONE COLOSSUS

By contrast with California the East Coast was seen as the home of a grittier, more basic style of jazz which toward the end of the 1950s came to be known as hard bop. As with cool jazz the term is easier to use than to define, but it is certainly true that the New York scene developed along very different lines. At the heart of it were two heavyweight tenors, Sonny Rollins (1930-) and John Coltrane (1926-67), and one middleweight, Hank Mobley (1930-86).

If jazz tenor style was still divided into Coleman Hawkins men and Lester Young men — and it was — then Rollins and Coltrane were both Hawkins men in that they worked through a song by extracting everything they could from its harmonies. Tape-recording and long-play records now allowed them to do this at considerable length.

Rollins's roots lie deep in bebop. In fact, if you play a Rollins LP at 45rpm it can sound uncannily like Charlie Parker. Rollins has always been happy to concentrate for material on the 12-bar blues and the 32-bar standard song, but what he can do with this basic material is tremendous. He is a strategist, a master of musical hide-and-seek. He begins with a simple tune — something like 'Surrey With A Fringe On Top' — then begins to twist and turn, delving deep into the harmonic intricacies, and just when the melody seems to have become lost for ever, up it pops again.

There is a great deal of humour in Rollins and enormous ingenuity in the shuffling of quite simple ideas into endless new shapes. He claims that he does this instinctively. Once, after reading a long analysis of one of his solos, he was unable to play for a week because it had made him too conscious of his

Selmer began life in France at the end of the 19th century when Henri Selmer, a fine clarinet player, set up a business producing, at first, clarinet reeds and mouthpieces. Then it progressed to the manufacture of clarinets. (The company's strange acoustic device, left, was designed in the 1920s to amplify a clarinet.) During the 1920s, after buying the Sax company, the Paris-based Selmer company began to produce saxophones, in line with the post-war boom in sax popularity. At first Selmer's saxes were unexceptional, such as the Model 22 shown in this British ad (below). However, with a series of innovative instruments that pleased players — and attracted the design departments of many other makers both in Europe and the United States — Selmer Paris gradually came to dominate the saxophone industry.

Multi-instrumental virtuoso Benny Carter (above) in 1936, the year he came to Europe as guest arranger for the BBC Dance Orchestra. Carter's pure tone and smooth technique set the standard for alto saxophonists at the time.

THE CHOICE OF THE ARTIST

The Banjo with the UNIQUE TONE CHAMBER.

The finest product of EUROPE

SELMER

The choice of a Saxophone rests always between some other make and—a Selmer. It is a brave man indeed who discards the Selmer when making his final choice, for here is a Saxophone that is something more than a name, a Saxophone that has found its way into every dance orchestra of repute and retained its place there.

If you do not at present play a Selmer, write for full particulars and prices. Easy payment arranged.

THE EPIPHONE RECORDING BANJO is the product of a new era in banjo. In tone, supreme. No other instrument can equal its carrying power, its flexibility and its range of expression. Its special tone chamber gives complete clarity of balanced sound. If you would learn more of this beautiful and modern banjo, write for full particulars and prices. Easy payments available.

J·R·LAFLEUR & SON·LTD
147 WARDOUR ST. LONDON. W.I.

For the Super Sax, Selmer had moved from their earlier saxophones, the Model 22 and Model 26, to a new-style instrument. The Super Sax seen in this 1932 ad (above), was also called the Super Model, but is known by players as the "Cigar Cutter" (see caption, far left). A distinctive Selmer feature is the wishbone-shape split strut leading to the octave key on the neck, first seen on the Super. (Other makers had a single strut.) Selmer used the gap in its split version to display a company identification badge.

Selmer Super Sax "Cigar Cutter" alto saxophone c1933 (right) By the time this Selmer Paris model appeared around 1930 the company had begun to make a mark. The Super Sax is usually known among players today as the "Cigar Cutter". The nickname comes from a small, purely decorative circular cut-out on the octave key post (not visible in this picture) that looks like the device used to cut cigars.

Selmer Mark VI tenor saxophone c1957 (right) The various Mark VI models quickly established themselves among players, especially jazz musicians, at the peak of Selmer Paris's post-war saxophone design. The Mark VI (named for its development from a sixth prototype) seemed artfully to combine all the finest Selmer features in a beautifully ergonomic instrument that has since attracted a great number of the leading saxophone players around the world. In the view of many saxophonists, Selmer have yet to improve upon the design. The Mark VI instruments were produced by Selmer Paris between 1954 and 1974, and are now collectable "vintage" items.

Sonny Rollins (above) produced in the 1950s some of the finest tenor saxophone albums of all time and then, to everyone's amazement, retired for almost three years to practice and develop his ideas. His 1961 comeback album, 'The Bridge' (inset), referred to his habit of practising on New York's Williamsburg Bridge. There was no great change in his style at first, but in subsequent years changes did gradually appear, particularly in his tone. He learned to change it at will, thick and solid at one moment, hollow the next, and sometimes spiced with the widest vibrato since Sidney Bechet. His public appearances in the 1980s and 90s have been marathon affairs, highly demanding in terms of both mental and physical stamina.

Marcel Mule, seen with a Selmer soprano in his Paris Saxophone Quartet in this 1950 ad (left), helped the company to design the Mark VI saxophone. Mule was born in 1902 in France and became a classical saxophone virtuoso. In the late 1920s he organised the military's Garde Républicaine band into a saxophone quartet, which later became the Paris Saxophone Quartet. They did much to publicise the instrument's classical potential. Mule taught classical saxophone at the Paris Conservatoire from 1942 to 1968, and his study materials are still in use today.

PARIS SAXOPHONE QUARTET
broadcasting with their
Selmer
instruments
THURSDAY, 4th MAY, 6—6.30 p.m. (THIRD PROGRAMME)
Marcel Mule, soprano; André Bauchy, alto; Georges Charron, tenor; Marcel Josse, baritone. These virtuosi, like their colleagues in the Paris Conservatoire and Garde Republicaine, play Selmer exclusively. Hear them and decide that Selmer will help you to fulfil your ambitions. The words "Selmer Sax" on a p.c. will bring you details.
Selmer 114, Charing Cross Road, London, W C.2

The Mark VI model made by Selmer was launched by the French company in the early 1950s, and its striking qualities soon caused a stir among players. Ads began to appear for the new instrument: this one (below left) from 1960 appeared in the American jazz magazine Down Beat, while the 1955 ad from the British musicians' newspaper Melody Maker (below right) urges readers to add their name to the waiting list for one of these sought-after new Selmers.

Selmer Mark VI alto saxophone c1962 (left) Selmer Paris's masterstroke, the Mark VI, first appeared in 1954. It achieved an ergonomic facility which many players still believe to be unsurpassed in modern saxophone design. The Mark VI built on the achievements of the Balanced Action and Super Action designs, adding a new octave mechanism and improvements to the bottom action. Selmer also added a couple of decorations that set the model apart. An "S" for Selmer emblem was added to the wishbone-shape octave key strut, and the thumbplate on the back of the body was given a more comfortable black plastic button. This Mark VI alto once belonged to the British bandleader Ivy Benson, who headed a renowned all-female big-band.

This is Stan Getz. His genius is improvisation: daring, nimble, brilliantly creative. "Focus," his album with Eddie Sauter, is already a jazz classic. Now, "Jazz Samba" creates a trend and sets its pace—the excitement of Bossa Nova. This is Stan Getz. Unique.

Hear him exclusively on **Verve**

Verve Records is a Division of Metro-Goldwyn-Mayer, Inc.

JAZZ SAMBA ‡ STAN GETZ ‡ CHARLIE BYRD

CONTAINS THE HIT SINGLE DESAFINADO!

V/V6-8432

Stan Getz [above], an early disciple of Lester Young, evolved a coolly romantic sound in the 1950s and found popular success with the Brazilian-jazz fusion style bossa nova. His 1962 album Jazz Samba with guitarist Charlie Byrd started a craze that lasted several years and saw Getz's singles 'Desafinado' and 'The Girl From Ipanema' trailing close behind the Beatles in the charts.

Paul Desmond [above], composer of 'Take Five' for Dave Brubeck's quartet, sought an alto saxophone tone 'like a dry Martini'.

A Selmer Paris factory worker is seen in this 1953 photograph (below) dealing with a stack of new saxophone bells intended for the company's Super Action model of the time.

Ben Webster (above) was one of the great original stylists of the tenor saxophone. He brought new life to the Ellington band in 1939. His driving,

Selmer Super Action alto saxophone c1949 (left) While Selmer's Balanced Action saxophone of the mid 1930s (see left) had introduced a redesigned key system and repositioned bell keys, the Super Action of 1948 went further with innovative offset keys, positioned to sit more comfortably under the player's hands. The Super Action was also the first saxophone with a detachable bell, which facilitated repairs and maintenance.

exterior, Webster was a romantic at heart. As he grew older this side of his personality blossomed, producing many breathy ballad masterpieces. He spent his last years in Europe and was on the point of taking Dutch citizenship when he died in 1973. His estate is administered by the Dutch Crown. But the saxophone was not the exclusive domain of jazz musicians. Like Ben Webster, the saxophonists of Henry Hall's BBC Dance Orchestra (inset), one of the finest and most versatile bands of its time, also played and endorsed Selmer instruments. The Selmer Balanced Action (or 'BA') was a superb instrument and, although it was replaced by the Mk VI in the 1950s, several leading jazz musicians, including Scott Hamilton and Bobby Wellins, still play the BA.

urgent solo on Duke's 'Cottontail' (1940) and the silky, insinuating 'Just A-Sittin' And A-Rockin'' (1941) are all-time classics. Under a tough, laconic

Selmer Super Action 80 Series II tenor saxophone c1996 (left) Selmer Paris seemed to be nearer the form that players expected from the company that had designed the Mark VI when they launched the Super Action Series II instruments in 1986. Possibly spurred by competition from Japanese makers, Selmer went for an easier response on the Series II, especially in the lower register. Recently Selmer have added a new Series III, in parallel with Series II, introducing a soprano and tenor in 1997. The alto was expected to be added during 1999. Selmer say that their new Series III model saxophones have better acoustic properties and improved airtightness, as well as further key layout changes.

After the Mark VI, Selmer brought out the ill-fated Mark VII in 1974 (see ad, above left). Although the Mark VII did have some changes for the good, most players seemed disappointed after the success of the Mark VI models and there were criticisms of a brighter sound and poorer feel. The Super Action 80 replaced the Mark VII in 1981 (ad, above right), and had a better feel to the key spacing, as well as a clever system of spring-loaded keywork.

Selmer US was established around 1900 as a distribution agency for Selmer Paris, but by the 1920s was producing its own instruments too, although none are of particular note.

Selmer Mark VI soprano saxophone c1971 (above) Despite John Coltrane, the Mark VI soprano was never as popular as the altos and tenors, mainly because it retained some surprisingly old-fashioned design aspects usually seen only on earlier saxophones.

57

own thought processes. Since then he has studiously avoided reading anything about himself in print. Between 1959 and 1961 Rollins took the unusual step of retiring from public performance in order to practice and work out new ideas. One of his favourite practice spots was on the walkway of the Williamsburg Bridge that crosses the East River to join Manhattan and Queens in New York City – a place where no one but the seagulls could hear him.

In recent years Rollins has become one of the few jazz saxophonists to use a microphone mounted on the bell of the instrument. It allows him to prowl around while playing. He also uses it to make brief announcements, which gives rise to the interesting spectacle of a man apparently talking to a saxophone. Like most of the great players, Rollins plays an instrument (an early Selmer Mark VI) that looks like something out of a museum of industrial archaeology. This is because all the lacquer has worn away – and musicians are reluctant to have saxophones relacquered. It involves separation from the instrument while the job is being done, and it is believed to affect the tone. Whatever the case, the more senior and distinguished the musician, the more disgusting-looking the instrument he plays. Shiny new saxophones are instantly suspect, and as for these modern confections tinted in pink, green or mauve... they are simply beyond the pale.

OLÉ COLTRANE

Although John Coltrane died in 1967 his influence is still powerfully at work in jazz today. It is practically impossible to find a tenor saxophonist below the age of 40 who does not to some extent echo his sound and approach. Coltrane had been a working musician since the late 1940s, but seemed suddenly to arrive when he joined the Miles Davis Quintet in 1955. At first he caused consternation. His metallic, unyielding tone and angular phrasing struck many listeners as being deliberately ugly, but there was also a massive authority about his musical presence that could not be denied.

It was during Coltrane's time with the Quintet that Miles Davis made a radical and far-reaching innovation in the approach to jazz improvisation by basing it not on sequences of chords but on scales, or "modes". This concept of modal improvisation suited Coltrane perfectly and set his musical course for the rest of his life. The chords (or "changes") of a standard tune move purposefully forward, following a logical path in a given number of bars. But a mode can go wandering on for ever, because it has no harmonic tension.

Modes, which are found in medieval plainsong and Indian ragas, are timeless and contemplative in character. Coltrane was a naturally thoughtful person, increasingly occupied in spiritual meditation. From 1959, when he formed his first quartet, until his death in 1967 his music echoes this cast of mind. Nonetheless, no one could deny Coltrane's skill in playing on changes when he chose. Indeed, his composition 'Giant Steps', recorded in 1959, is still regarded as the hardest chord sequence to play on and is regularly used as a test-piece by student saxophonists.

It probably says something profound about the way music reflects deep attitudes in society that John Coltrane's essentially static modal music took over so completely during the 1960s from the forward-moving, active, optimistic, chord-based jazz of bebop and before.

It was Coltrane too who revived the soprano saxophone, at almost the precise moment that the instrument's first great pioneer Sidney Bechet died. In Coltrane's hands it could have been a different instrument from the one played by Bechet and Johnny Hodges. Coltrane developed a level, piping tone that at times can almost be mistaken for an oboe or maybe some kind of oriental folk instrument. The sound became widely known through Coltrane's recorded version of 'My Favorite Things', altered to fit into a modal framework and the cause of a sensation in the jazz world in 1960. A lot of old Bechet and Hodges fans hated it. The jazz-loving poet Philip Larkin said that what he called the "thin drizzle" of Coltrane's soprano playing put him in mind of a club bore who had been magically transformed into a set of bagpipes.

Soprano saxophonist Steve Lacy, who had worked with Jimmy Giuffre and Thelonius Monk among others before forming his own bands in the early 1960s, was the primary influence on Coltrane's decision to move to soprano. Lacy wrote in *Metronome* in 1961: "Coltrane was looking for a relief and contrast to his tenor and also an extension of the higher register, and found it quite naturally in the soprano, which is both in the same key and exactly one octave higher than the tenor. His playing combines great harmonic complexity, a dry, almost Eastern sound and unflagging propulsion, which when used in his present format (sometimes with two basses droning hypnotically) produces quite an exotic mood."

If you could take a look at the books of an instrument manufacturer of the 1960s and 1970s you would be bound to see a phenomenal increase in the number of soprano saxophones produced by their factory. Following Coltrane's lead, jazz tenor players began turning more and more to the soprano as their second instrument. It was not a simple undertaking. For various technical acoustic reasons that we won't go into here, the soprano saxophone is a difficult instrument to play in tune, and switching from tenor to soprano and back again tends only to make the problem worse. It bothered Coltrane himself so much that in the end he settled for playing whole sets on one or the other.

Coltrane had outlined some of the problems of the instrument to Don DeMichael in *Down Beat* at the end of 1960. "I like the sound of [my new soprano]," Coltrane said, "but I'm not playing with the body, the bigness of tone, that I want yet. I haven't had too much trouble playing in tune, but I've had a lot of trouble getting a good quality of tone in the upper register. It comes out sort of puny sometimes. I've had to adopt a slightly different approach than the one I use for tenor, but it helps me get away — lets me take another look at improvisation. It's like having another hand."

In their different ways, both Rollins and Coltrane were vehement, determined, rigorous men, and their playing showed it. They left no stone unturned as they ploughed their way through their solos. In fact Coltrane's solos were so dense in texture that critics began to describe them as "sheets of sound". This was the Hawkins method. Hank Mobley, on the other hand, was elegant, quietly witty and said what he had to say in as few notes as possible — a spiritual descendant of Lester Young, in other words.

Mobley followed Coltrane into the Miles Davis Quintet, although Miles never liked him and omitted virtually all mention of him from the trumpeter's highly detailed autobiography. Some of Mobley's solos with Miles are gems of poise and ingenuity, but he plays them with such modesty and lack of swagger that they can easily be overlooked. Mobley's best work can be heard on his albums for the Blue Note label made in the early 1960s shortly after leaving the Quintet, especially his masterpiece *Soul Station*. Mobley's later albums suffer from an excess of soul-jazz numbers and even the inclusion of Motown tunes, presumably in an effort to inject an element of fashion and a bit of dash into the proceedings.

KIND OF CANNONBALL

When Charlie Parker died in March 1955, alto saxophone style was left bobbing in his wake. The two most obvious inheritors of Parker's mantle were Phil Woods (1931-) and Jackie McLean (1932-), but a newcomer from Florida turned up in New York later that year and upset the entire picture.

Julian "Cannonball" Adderley (1928-75) possessed a phenomenal technique. Although the inescapable influence of Parker was obvious enough in his playing, there was something different about it: a kind of strutting, down-home simplicity beneath the torrents of notes. Adderley joined Coltrane in Miles Davis's band for a while, turning it from a quintet into a sextet. He played on the classic *Kind Of Blue* album in 1959 and then went on to form his own band that included in the line-up Cannonball's cornet-playing brother, Nat.

This band, along with the Horace Silver Quintet, headed the soul-jazz movement of the late 1950s and early 1960s. Borrowing phrases, harmonies, rhythms and even handclaps from the Southern Baptist church, along with references to black everyday life and speech, Adderley, Silver and a few others anticipated the soul music explosion that happened a few years later.

In retrospect the later 1950s proved to be a golden age for jazz. Not only were contemporary players like Rollins, Coltrane and Adderley reaching their early maturity, but virtually all of the heroes of earlier periods were still alive and playing. Ben Webster, for instance, had reached a peak of blowsy perfection. Dexter Gordon began recording a superb series of albums for Blue Note, far better than anything he had done before, and Coleman Hawkins was performing with undimmed brilliance. Only Lester Young, sick and disheartened, was failing; he died in 1959. His followers of the Four Brothers school also found themselves out of favour, and Stan Getz removed himself temporarily to live and work in Denmark.

Up until this moment, through all the developments and stylistic upsets, jazz had been sustained by one agreed and inviolable rule: all improvisation had to be *on* something, almost always the harmonies of the original tune, and it had to

59

Hank Mobley (right), the 'Middleweight Champion' of the tenor, reached his peak in the late 1950s and early 60s. Curiously, much of the music he recorded at the time was not released until after his death in 1986. The excellent 'Faraway Lands' is one of these posthumous releases. Its cover shows Mobley and the King Super-20 tenor that he was then playing. At other times he played a Selmer Mk VI.

Coltrane played Selmer Mk VI tenor (right) and soprano saxophones. The Mk VI range, introduced in the 1950s, quickly became the most popular of all instruments with professional players. The fact that it was chosen by artists as eminent as Coltrane and Rollins was sufficient recommendation for most. The instrument is highly prized today and it is rare to find a Selmer Mk VI advertised for sale.

Julian 'Cannonball' Adderley (above and left) arrived in New York from his native Florida shortly after the death of Charlie Parker and soon gained the status of leading altoist. After a period with Miles Davis he formed his own phenomenally successful quintet with his brother, Nat, on cornet. The Adderley Brothers played catchy soul-jazz numbers like 'Dis Here' and 'Sack O' Woe'. Cannonball played and endorsed King Super-20 saxophones.

John Coltrane (left) brought a whole new sensibility to jazz. His long, wide-ranging solos, the unremitting pressure behind his improvisation, the steely tone and urgent attack caused consternation when he first appeared as a member of the Miles Davis Quintet. He was also capable of tender ballad playing, but this aspect was increasingly overshadowed as his career progressed. The speed and complexity of Coltrane's mature style led one critic to describe it as 'sheets of sound', with individual notes barely distinguishable. The album 'Giant Steps', released in 1960, was an instant classic, and has never been out of print. It was the first Coltrane record to consist entirely of original compositions, including the fiendishly difficult title piece. 'My Favourite Things', recorded in the same year, introduced Coltrane's soprano playing and sparked a revival of this neglected

instrument, featured in a version of Cole Porter's 'Ev'ry Time We Say Goodbye'. This was the start of Coltrane's association with pianist McCoy Tyner and drummer Elvin Jones, who, with bassist Reggie Workman, made up the classic John Coltrane Quartet.

be contained within a structure, usually the 12-bar blues or 32-bar song. You could say that it was like a painting or sculpture having to be *of* something, a representation of a subject, however distorted the result might be. Now along came a generation of jazz musicians who challenged this fundamental tenet and introduced the jazz equivalent of abstract art. The musician who made the first sensational move was the alto saxophonist Ornette Coleman (1930-).

DANCING IN YOUR HEAD

Whereas Charlie Parker would establish a theme, trace solos through the chord sequence, and tie it up with the tune again at the end, Coleman and his trumpet partner Don Cherry seemed to skate off at illogical tangents, pursuing a melodic idea with little or no regard for the harmony. Many listeners, by no means all cloth-eared, simply gave up.

For years before he was ever recorded, Coleman had been playing this way. He had worked the R&B circuit in Texas and the south-west playing with little bands to audiences who knew exactly what they wanted – and whatever it was, it wasn't free improvisation. But Coleman seemed driven by some personal demon that he was powerless to control.

The titles of his early records made a point of telling everyone that here was the musical future: *Something Else!* and *The Shape Of Jazz To Come* and *Change Of The Century*. The extent to which listeners accepted the music depended on what they enjoyed about jazz in the first place. Those who were attracted by the self-expression and the iconoclastic, anti-establishment approach welcomed Coleman warmly. Those who liked the swing and intimacy and wit of jazz couldn't take him at any price. This sort of thing had happened before in both jazz and classical music, but most people eventually came around. In the case of free jazz, however, some kind of critical point seemed to have been reached. Getting on for 40 years later there are many listeners with broad tastes whose enjoyment of jazz stops dead with Ornette Coleman.

On his early records Coleman played a Grafton Acrylic saxophone – not like Charlie Parker had done as a matter of expediency, but because he liked it. He bought his first one in Los Angeles in 1954, initially because it was cheap and all he could afford. In 1961 he told writer Nat Hentoff: "I didn't like it at first, but I figured it would be better to have a new horn

anyway. Now I won't play any other. They're made in England and I have to send for them. They're only good for a year the way I play them." Coleman believed that the plastic instrument had a special tone quality and produced "purer notes". How he contrived to get through a saxophone a year remains a mystery. In any case, 1961 was Grafton's final year of production, so he was obliged to settle for a conventional instrument from the mid 1960s onwards.

Poised midway between post-Parker hard bop and the free-form jazz of Ornette Coleman stands the unique Eric Dolphy (1928-64), a multi-talented virtuoso of the alto saxophone, bass clarinet and flute. His usual method was to work within the traditional structures of harmony and chorus-lengths but to push against them like a man struggling to fight his way out of a huge paper bag.

Although he died after only about six years in the jazz limelight, Dolphy remains an influential figure because of his distinctly personal and convincing style as well as his sheer brilliance as an instrumentalist.

It is probably no coincidence that free jazz expanded so quickly in the 1960s. The spirit of the age itself favoured revolutionary statements and artistic experiment. But this was also the decade in which jazz lost the bulk of its truly popular base. The general public no longer paid any attention, so jazz musicians no longer took the trouble to please it. The already divided jazz audience shrank to a collection of coteries, each with its little segment to defend.

Only in such a situation could players like Albert Ayler (1936-70) have flourished. Ayler's banshee howls and shrieks attracted a good deal of serious attention during the mid 1960s, and his 1964 album *Spiritual Unity* has been described as "the fiercest and most uncompromising sax playing on record". Which leads one to ask: "Uncompromising with what? The human ear? Common sense?"

The figure who stood up as principal spokesman for free jazz was tenor saxophonist Archie Shepp (1937-), an articulate man with an academic background who also wrote plays. Shepp cleverly exploited the term "freedom" in such a way that it could refer to both musical freedom (the absence of restraining forms) and political freedom. He habitually referred to himself as being "in the tradition of" Hawkins, Young, Parker and so on, and because he said it so often and so loudly critics and the public were numbed into taking him at his own estimation. The masters with whom Shepp claimed kinship were either dead or past caring and therefore unlikely to protest. Shepp's early work leaned heavily on "collective improvisation" (everybody blowing at once) but he later turned to playing conventional material in a lumpish and thoroughly uncharming manner.

However, an assumption that jazz had permanently lost its popular audience would be unnecessarily gloomy. Certainly the masses were unlikely to take Ayler or Shepp to their hearts, but there were other choices. One was the organ-and-saxophone combo music still enjoyed by the patrons of bars in Harlem and other places. Altoist Lou Donaldson (1926-) and tenorist Stanley Turrentine (1934-) were long-standing masters of this unpretentious but essentially happy genre which specialised in numbers with revealing titles such as 'Midnight Creeper', 'Hot Dog' and 'Alligator Boogaloo'.

In 1961 Stan Getz returned to the US from Scandinavia to find his own style eclipsed and free jazz in the ascendant. Casting around for some new stimulus he looked into the small but growing interest among American jazz musicians in contemporary Brazilian popular song.

The interest was mutual; the new songwriters in Rio were fascinated by the harmonies and phrasing of West Coast jazz. In the space of one day in February 1962 Getz recorded *Jazz Samba*, an entire album of modern Brazilian tunes, with guitarist Charlie Byrd's group. Out of it came the enormously successful hit single 'Desafinado' and, ultimately, the whole phenomenon known as bossa nova. As a popular craze bossa nova lasted less than three years, but it provided a permanent addition to the jazz language and contributed at least one masterpiece, the 1964 album *Getz/Gilberto* where Getz collaborated with Brazilian singer/guitarist Joao Gilberto. These sessions spawned another hit, 'The Girl From Ipanema', with Gilberto's wife Astrud on vocals.

The 1960s also saw the advent of the unique Roland Kirk (1936-77), one of the most remarkable figures in the whole history of jazz and a man who could do anything with a saxophone short of eating it. Not only did he regularly play three at once, but also he actually managed to invent his own instruments by redesigning earlier, defunct varieties in order to suit his very particular musical requirements. Kirk's three

main instruments, often played simultaneously, were the tenor saxophone (a modified King Super-20), the manzello and the stritch. The manzello was Kirk's adaptation of the saxello, a semi-curved soprano made by King in the 1920s. The stritch was originally an alto with a straight body, like an enormous, eccentric soprano, and this too Kirk modified for his own use.

In playing two or three instruments at once he could never have both hands on one instrument at any one time, so each of his saxes had additional keywork fitted to enable him to play one-handed (or even occasionally no-handed). The results looked thoroughly peculiar, with rods and levers and bits of cork sticking out at all angles. But the appearance did not concern Kirk, who was blind. He had considered everything carefully and instructed a technician in exactly what he wanted. Nor was this the end of the matter. At the age of 39 Kirk suffered a stroke which paralysed one side of his body. Undeterred, he redesigned his tenor saxophone's keywork to one-handed operation and carried on playing until his death, 18 months later.

The tale of Roland Kirk says a great deal about that astounding man, the brilliance of his mind and the strength of his will. It also says a great deal about the saxophone, because no other instrument in the world would have stood up to an assault of that kind. Anything else would have gone wildly out of tune, lost great tracts of its range, or simply collapsed. But the saxophone, the despised former novelty instrument of dubious parentage, sang Roland Kirk's song sweetly and without complaint.

SHORTER FUSE

In the later 1960s jazz found some common ground with the prevailing rock idiom. The direction was pointed out once again by Miles Davis, in a series of albums beginning with *Filles de Kilimanjaro* in 1968 and leading a year or so later through *In A Silent Way* to *Bitches Brew*, his first fully developed jazz-rock fusion album.

The saxophonist with Miles throughout this period was Wayne Shorter (1933-) who had begun as a hard-bopper with Art Blakey's Jazz Messengers and gradually evolved a personal style that owed something to Coltrane, only more gentle in conception and softer in tone. In 1970 Shorter left Miles to form the band Weather Report in partnership with pianist Joe

Ornette Coleman bought one of the few plastic-bodied Grafton saxophones (left) to be imported into the US. By this time (late 1950s) the production line had closed and Graftons were being hand-assembled from left-over parts. Coleman ordered a new one each year, until the supply finally dried up.

Ornette Coleman
Free Jazz

LP 1364

White saxophones obviously attract Ornette Coleman. Here he is (above) in 1994 with a white-enamelled Selmer. The title of his 1960 album 'Free Jazz' became the brand-name for his style of abstract improvisation and the whole jazz movement that followed in his wake. The arrival of free jazz created a permanent divide in the jazz audience.

Archie Shepp (above) initially followed Ornette Coleman's free jazz path, combining the music with revolutionary political rhetoric. Later he turned to more conventionally structured playing and also took up singing, concentrating on the blues.

King Saxello c1925 (right) was one of many experiments in shape tried out by instrument makers in the 1920s. It was a soprano with a half-crook at the mouthpiece end and an unturned bell. Of all the saxophones, the soprano is the one whose shape has never really settled down. It still comes in three basic configurations. A semi-curved alto never caught on because it was too awkward to to hold. Roland Kirk had modifications made to the saxello and renamed it the 'manzello'. Similarly, he modified the semi-curved alto, which he then called the 'stritch'.

Amazing: Rahsaan Roland Kirk in action (above). The saxophones, reading left to right, are manzello, stritch and tenor (King Super-20 Silversonic). Also visible is an assortment of whistles and a siren with horn attached. In addition, he regularly used flute, clarinet, nose-flute, stylophone, hi-hat cymbals and a gong. He claimed that the idea of playing three instruments at once came to him in a dream. Although at first he was dismissed as a novelty act, it gradually became obvious that he was a unique artist with a uniquely comprehensive grasp of the jazz tradition. He could play in virtually any style, moving from New Orleans march to bebop to rhythm & blues in the same performance. Although he was blind, Kirk was a great showman and knew exactly how to keep an audience guessing what astonishing feat he would bring off next. One critic aptly described him as combining the raw energy of a street enertainer with the extreme sophistication of a schooled modern jazz musician.

The saxello was made by H.N White, and bore its King banner (left) engraved on the bell. The semi-curved alto was made by the Buescher company.

65

Zawinul. As Weather Report's style matured the group sound took precedence over individual solo work and Shorter's tenor or soprano was often submerged in the mix; the records he made under his own name at around the same time show him to better effect.

Other tenor saxophonists whose names surfaced through jazz-rock in the late 1960s include Charles Lloyd (1938-) and Michael Brecker (1949-). Lloyd's somewhat indiscriminate mixture of modal tunes, rock rhythms, churchy soul numbers and funky blues, all delivered with a Coltrane-derived vehemence, brought him enormous popularity in the hippie era, packing vast auditoriums such as The Fillmore and sending him on numerous overseas tours.

Brecker's career actually began in jazz-rock. At the age of 21 he was a member of the fusion band Dreams and played in backing bands for James Taylor, Yoko Ono and others. As his playing matured it grew in breadth and technical command until by the end of the 1970s Brecker was being hailed as the finest tenor saxophonist of his generation. Young players increasingly took Brecker as their initial model, reaching back through him to Coltrane who was one of his own primary influences. Indeed it was Brecker who established the all-purpose contemporary tenor saxophone style, designed to be acceptable in more or less any context: jazz-rock, latter-day hard bop, big band, Latin.

The commonly-heard and largely justified complaint that "all these young tenor players sound alike" usually means that they all sound like Michael Brecker, or try to. He seems to have no weak spots, no quirks or oddities, just a stream of beautifully-turned, high-octane phrases delivered with seamless technique and a sound like polished glass. It is unfair to blame Brecker for being so good that everyone wants to copy him, but his influence has certainly helped along the process by which all the luxuriant variety of jazz is slowly being reduced to a single standard product.

NORDIC STONES AND RURAL SOUNDSCAPES

Meanwhile, free music was expanding into a new world of possibilities. Most of the later developments actually took it further away from jazz, but their first inspiration was obviously in the free jazz pioneered by Ornette Coleman. Europe played a big part in this. For instance, the Norwegian saxophonist Jan

Garbarek (1947-) started out as a teenage Coltrane fan and gradually developed a distinctive musical voice that could only be at home in a Nordic country. His was a clear, slightly chilly modal style with a tone of great purity and an aura suggestive of ancient stones and half-forgotten rituals. Similarly the British baritone and soprano saxophonist John Surman (1944-) is a West Countryman who creates effective rural soundscapes that could easily be used as illustrations to a novel by Thomas Hardy.

Others have developed more severely abstract music. Anthony Braxton (1945-) is an American who has done much of his best work in Europe. He sometimes uses mathematical formulae as the basis for his compositions and has occasionally been accused of taking an over-intellectual approach. His music is, however, full of dry humour. Braxton also regularly plays instruments from the extreme ends of the saxophone spectrum, such as the relatively tiny sopranino, the large bass and the enormous contra-bass.

Evan Parker (1944-) invented a new musical language for the saxophone, incorporating harmonics (notes above the normal range), multiphonics (producing two or more notes at once) and many other unconventional tones and textures. Parker is also a master of the art of circular breathing, a practice that has been employed occasionally by a number of players throughout jazz history.

Both Harry Carney and Roland Kirk used circular breathing extensively. Essentially it is the technique of blowing out and breathing in at the same time – which is not as absurd as it seems. While blowing a note, you allow your cheeks to fill with air; you then push that air out by closing your cheeks like a bellows, at the same time snatching a breath through your nose. With practice, it is possible to keep a constant stream of air going. On a single note it is fairly easy; the difficulty comes when you have other things to attend to at the same time.

The hard bop of the late 1950s resurfaced in the early 1980s to become what might be called the modern mainstream, quite separate from both fusion and free jazz. Records made by some musicians born in the late 1950s and 1960s can sound almost as though they were recorded before they were born.

Among them are a number of quite exceptional players including the tenor saxophonists Ralph Moore (1956-), Branford Marsalis (1960-) and Joshua Redman (1969-). None of them is untouched by the Coltrane influence, but they all cultivate a warmer, rounder tone and more supple phrasing. Both Rollins and Mobley have also clearly made their mark. On alto probably the finest modern mainstream player in the world today is Britain's Peter King (1940-). Although King is just old enough to have been an original hard bop man, his playing has grown and matured to an astonishing degree over the past 20 years, and his ability to construct long, intricate but thoroughly lucid lines is unsurpassed.

Through the 1980s and 1990s jazz has followed the pattern of pop music and split itself into a collection of ever-smaller segments, each with its own following. So specialised and exclusive have these become that there is no one today who would claim to enjoy jazz in all its manifestations.

A musician can be a style-leader in one segment yet their name may raise not even a flicker of recognition among adherents of another. A good example of one such mini-genre is M-Base, a fusion form in which jazz is allied with hip-hop and rap. Among its leading figures are the alto saxophonists Steve Coleman (1956-) and Greg Osby (1960-). They both started out in the stylistic shadow of Cannonball Adderley, later veering in the direction of latter-day funk stylists such as Maceo Parker (1943-).

At the other end of the spectrum comes the neo-classical or modern swing school. Outstanding here is the tenor saxophonist Scott Hamilton (1954-). When he first appeared in the early 1970s Hamilton was noted more as a phenomenon than for the quality of his playing. It was regarded as odd in the extreme that a young man barely out of his teens should be playing in the style of the 1940s, apparently finding himself quite at home in a musical genre dating from before his birth. Hamilton started as a fairly close approximation to Ben Webster, but his playing has matured over the ensuing decades into a highly personal voice, still rooted in swing but with the occasional light touch of bebop.

Other leading neo-classical tenor saxophonists are Harry Allen (1966-) and Ken Peplowski (1959-), the latter a clarinet virtuoso. There is a strange inconsistency about critical attitudes in this area. Hamilton and company are often either ignored or dismissed as revivalists by critics, whereas the modern mainstream school of Joshua Redman and company receives serious attention. Common sense would suggest that a

musician born in the 1950s and playing in the tradition of Ben Webster is in exactly the same position as one born in the 1960s playing in a style derived from John Coltrane.

Hamilton always plays a vintage saxophone, his favourite being a Selmer Balanced Action dating from the 1940s. He finds that modern instruments are faster, but that it is impossible to produce a really weighty tone with them. It is certainly true that up until the end of the 1960s wind instruments were not designed to be reliant on amplification, whereas those produced more recently are far more flimsy and lack carrying power. Today, serious young players of whatever style are likely to seek out a venerable Selmer Mark VI or King Super-20 to be their life's companion.

AIR SAXOPHONE

The popularity of the saxophone has risen and fallen with the popularity of jazz itself. As we have seen, there was a great vogue for it in the 1920s and it continued to be quite popular through the 1930s. During the war years and into the 1950s the accordion took over, while from the mid 1960s to the early 1980s the jazz influence on popular music was small and saxophones were not much in evidence. The attractive solo instrument of the moment was the guitar. Then in the mid 1980s fashion swung back again. Jazz of various kinds attracted a new audience and people once more began to want to play the saxophone.

The popularity of an instrument depends partly on its attractiveness to would-be players — its pose value, if you like. When middle-aged men play air guitar or pose in front of the mirror as they finger their Fender Strat they are indulging in a harmless fantasy derived from the glamour figures of their youth during the 1960s. Younger ones are just as likely to play air saxophone or trumpet, or pose with their shiny new saxophone of dubious eastern-European origin.

The ultimate test of popularity for an instrument comes with the attention of thieves. A few years ago one musical instrument store owner, whose premises had been broken into repeatedly over the years, reported that for the past couple of decades the robbers had taken guitars and left everything else. But this time, he said, they had left the guitars and stolen all the saxophones. No doubt somewhere Adolphe Sax and Sidney Bechet shared a smile.

Greg Osby (right), a prominent figure on the M-Base scene, determined to keep jazz in contact with contemporary popular culture.

On his newest JMT release "Season of Renewal". Greg plays V5 mouthpieces (A45 & S35), with 31/2 Java alto reeds and 3 soprano reeds.

Combining the language of the street with a new way of thinking, Greg Osby is a significant player in the new language of M-Base. His lyrical sound and style prompted Musician Magazine to say, "Osby may be the best ballad player of his generation." All the way to the top, Greg plays Vandoren reeds and mouthpieces because there is no substitute for the best. It's basic...M-Basic...

Great Players Play... **V** *Vandoren* PARIS

Sole US importer • J. D'Addario & Co.

Selmer Mark VI tenor saxophone c1957 (left)

M-Base (above) stands for 'Macro-Basic Array of Structured Extemporization', which in turn refers to an informal group of musicians devoted to seeking new fusions between jazz-influenced idioms such as rap, hip-hop and soul. Members include saxophonist Steve Coleman, pianist Geri Allen and vocalist Cassandra Wilson.

Michael Brecker (left), the most widely influential saxophonist of the 1980s and beyond. With his brother Randy, a trumpeter, he co-led the phenomenally successful Brecker Brothers band, toured with Steps and Steps Ahead, and became the first-choice saxophonist on every pop album. Brecker's playing is staggeringly accomplished and his invention never runs dry. In 1980 he took up the Electronic Wind Instrument (EWI), a form of synthesizer with saxophone fingering and a mouthpiece. He is now its leading exponent, closely followed by Britain's Phil Todd. The 1992 album 'Return Of The Brecker Brothers' features the EWI extensively.

BLINDFOLD TEST: Danny Gottlieb   For Contemporary Musicians

down beat

June, 1997 $1.75 U.K. £2.00

EDDIE DANIELS Clarinetist For All Seasons

10th Annual Student Music Awards

MICHAEL BRECKER

New Axe, New Attitude

BERNARD EDWARDS Hit Man On The Production Line

Anthony Braxton (left with bass saxophone) makes a point of playing the complete range of saxophones. He is a graduate in both music and philosophy, and once earned his living by playing chess for money in New York's Washington Square. His work is severely abstract, in both improvised and composed idioms, and is sometimes based on mathematical formulae. Braxton is one of the few saxophonists to give completely solo recitals. By contrast, Ken Peplowski, Scott Hamilton and Spike Robinson (below left) follow the mainstream. Their styles derive from such great originals of jazz tenor as Lester Young and Ben Webster. Collectively, this school of jazz is sometimes known as 'neo-classic'. It has a strong following in Britain and northern Europe.

SCoTT HaMiLToN
KeN PePLoWSKi GRooViN' HiGH
SPiKe RoBiNSoN

Joshua Redman (right), son of saxophonist Dewey Redman, having graduated with top honours from Harvard, was intending to become a lawyer. In 1991, just for curiosity, he entered the Thelonious Monk competition for young jazz musicians - and won. He signed a recording contract with Warner Brothers and embarked on an unexpected career. Redman plays tenor in a swinging, lucid, melodic style that appeals to jazz lovers of diverse tastes. He appears in the 1996 film 'Kansas City', playing the part of Lester Young in a jam session scene.

Norwegian saxophonist-composer Jan Garbarek (above) began as a Coltrane follower, but developed a style that draws on his Nordic roots and other folk sources. In 1970 Garbarek's debut album launched the successful German label ECM.

POP SAXOPHONE AND BRASS

by Paul Trynka

Louis Jordan paved the way for rock'n'roll, and soon Fats Domino was relying on New Orleans horn sections and Frank Sinatra was concocting sophisticated wind-assisted pop. The Beatles and The Beach Boys coloured their ever-complex rock arrangements with brass, and the sax agitated at the heart of vibrant funk and steaming soul, while to earn its keep today a living, breathing instrument must outperform the digital sampler.

AS POPULAR MUSIC BURGEONED after World War II, players of saxophones, woodwind and brass instruments constituted a vital cornerstone of Western culture. They were the most esteemed players in the big-bands popular at the time, while guitarists and the rhythm section were seen as indisputably of a lower class – despite the efforts of drummer Gene Krupa or guitarist Charlie Christian.

Hundreds of "territory bands" enjoyed lucrative regional empires in the more far-flung American states, while there was a vibrant session and live scene in regional centres such as Los Angeles, New York, Chicago and New Orleans.

Thanks to a combination of factors, music was changing fast, and the foundations of what we now know as rock music were all in place. In a time of exciting growth and change, the position of sax and brass players looked unassailable.

ROCK'N'ROLL ROOTS

Rock'n'roll emerged through a complex set of origins and influences, but the musics from which it sprang relied heavily on wind instruments. Most people would describe black R&B and white country as integral parts of rock'n'roll's make-up, and while the saxophone was already one of the prime instruments in R&B, it was also starting to make its presence

felt in country music. Country – or hillbilly as it was often originally termed – started out with basic guitar-based bands, but its scope and instrumentation expanded as it developed into western swing, a significant precursor of rock'n'roll.

Probably the most important country ensemble to influence rock'n'roll was Bob Wills & His Texas Playboys. Wills, a fiddle player, had used a straightforward hillbilly line-up for his first bands, but by 1935 had recruited Art Haines, who doubled on fiddle and trombone, trumpet player Everett Stover, and Robert "Zeb" McNally on tenor or alto saxophone. Wills's band was probably the hottest thing on white radio throughout the 1930s and 1940s, but when veteran Capitol producer Art Satherley was brought in to record the band in 1935, he was staggered at the presence in Wills's band of the horn section, and told the bandleader, "We do not want any horns." Wills replied, "I got along before I met you fellas, and I will still get along. I will either record with horns, or I'm going back to Tulsa."

As time went on Wills employed even bigger horn sections which at times stretched to four or five reeds, trombone and two trumpets. The nucleus of his line-up, perhaps nine musicians, would include two saxes and one trumpet. While Spade Cooley's western swing band at one time numbered 24 men, Wills's model proved the more affordable and was used by many more of the western swing bands that followed in Wills's wake, perhaps most notably Bill Haley's Saddlemen, who would later become legendary as The Comets. There are many who contend that the music of Bob Wills and of his brilliant contemporary Louis Jordan was, in effect, rock'n'roll. The work of these two gifted bandleaders certainly contained most of rock'n'roll's prime elements. Wills, like Jordan, was already mixing black and white traditions in his music, incorporating blues, jazz and even Mexican-influenced material into his repertoire, and his love for black music traditions ran deep – he'd learnt songs from black musicians in his youth and revered blues singer Bessie Smith.

But where rock'n'roll would revel in simplicity, Wills was dedicated to exploring more and more complex arrangements. By 1940 when he recorded with an 18-piece band Wills had moved from his guitar-led and fiddle-dominated origins to almost pure swing music, recording 'New San Antonio Rose' with an eight-piece horn section. It was his biggest hit to date, and provided a profound indication of the breaking down of barriers between supposedly separate forms like jazz and country. Saxophonist Zeb McNally was by this point effectively the leader of Wills's outfit, responsible for administering fines or other punishments to errant Playboys, underlining the fact that by now the saxophone was as important a part of the band's sound as the guitar or fiddle.

There was one famous performer who was an even more profound influence on rock'n'roll: Louis Jordan (1908-75). He first made his reputation playing alto saxophone with bandleader and drummer Chick Webb, who recorded a run of pop/jazz hits after recruiting vocalist Ella Fitzgerald to his outfit in 1935. Once Jordan signed a solo deal with Decca in 1938 he established a small band which he named the Tympany Five after his shortlived enthusiasm for incorporating timpani drums into his sound.

Working with a variety of witty, catchy pieces like 'Caldonia' that were largely self-penned, Jordan became supremely accomplished at exploiting the rhythmic potential of his compact line-up, specialising in infectious shuffles. Around 1945 he recruited electric guitarist Carl Hogan who helped make up a seven-strong unit that retained the Tympany Five name. Hogan's presence increased the outfit's impact on rock'n'roll: both Jordan and Hogan were cited by rock'n'roll's

most gifted songwriter, Chuck Berry, as the prime influence on his career. Throughout the 1940s Jordan racked up hit after hit: 'GI Jive', 'Ain't Nobody Here But Us Chickens', 'Choo Choo Ch'Boogie' and more, many of them simultaneous hits on the R&B and pop charts, anticipating the impact of Berry.

Louis Jordan had a firm grasp of what would make a hit record, and lengthy sax solos were rarely called for. However, his use of the horn section for both rhythm and lead licks anticipated the soul horn sections of the 1960s, while his overall sound incorporated all the musical elements of rock'n'roll. Although Jordan generally used his alto sax as a complement to the lead vocal, rather than for extensive soloing, he was no mean player. He dabbled with baritone, soprano and tenor sax, but his most exciting playing was without doubt on the alto. Jazz saxophonist Sonny Rollins was one of many admirers of Jordan's technique: "He had a great big sound on the alto," said Rollins, "and I just loved him." Around 1970, in Jordan's twilight years, he recorded with Chicago guitarists Dave and Louis Myers a series of instrumentals for the French Black & Blue label which demonstrated his soloing skills.

BIG JAY AND THE EARL

Jordan's music typified the jump blues which was evolving during the 1940s. This dance-oriented black music provided a valuable antidote to the bland pop which seemed to have taken over after the big-bands' heyday. Along with Jordan, other performers crossed over to the pop scene, anticipating the seismic influence of rock'n'roll. Big Jay McNeely (1927-) was one of a number of R&B performers attracting frenetic white audiences in the pre-rock'n'roll era. McNeely's boisterous, rhythmic tenor sax instrumentals were matched by his on-stage flamboyance. He'd work his young audiences to a frenzy with extravagant antics such as playing sax while rolling on the floor. McNeely first recorded for Federal in 1946 and over the next five years scored a string of R&B hits, drawing bigger and bigger white audiences while attracting increasing scorn from musicians schooled in the sophisticated big-bands.

Earl Bostic (1913-65), who boasted rather better musical credentials, was another alto saxophone player who became famous with a small combo. Bostic had played with jazz bandleaders such as Lionel Hampton and Cab Calloway, but his solo hits like 1951's 'Flamingo' were a success with young

Couesnon alto saxophone c1910 (right) Couesnon was one of a handful of French makers who began building saxophones around 1900 following Adolphe Sax's developments. The rockers of the 1950s may have started on ancient horns of this sort, but most would have found that contemporary instruments were preferable.

Louis Jordan and his Tympany Five (below and right) Once a sideman with Chick Webb, Jordan dispensed with his original tympani-led band and developed a distinctive sound which hugely influenced rock'n'roll. The 1941 advertisement for King saxophones (below) credits 'Louie Jordan' as leader of the 'Tympanni Five', then playing a Chicago residence, and reflects a general confusion about the name and spelling

of his band, which usually included six or seven musicians. A superb innovator in popular music, Jordan played succinctly on alto, tenor and baritone sax but was generally overlooked. Sonny Rollins, however, admired him.

Bob Wills And His Texas Playboys (above) Before the arrival of Western swing pioneer Bob Wills, horn sections were unknown in country music. This 1940s Playboys line-up includes, from the left, long-term sideman Zeb McNally (alto sax), Everett Stover (trumpet), Joe Ferguson (tenor), Tubby Lewis (trumpet) and Tiny Mott (tenor). Wills is holding the fiddle.

Earl Bostic (left) Classically trained, Bostic played with Cab Calloway, Gene Krupa and Lionel Hampton. After signing to King, Bostic recorded a series of instrumentals, such as 1951's 'Flamingo', which were hits with both black and white audiences. His jazz credibility did not suffer. John Coltrane, who graduated from Bostic's band, commented: "He had fantastic technical abilities, and showed me many a trick."

73

Big Jay McNeely (left) McNeely's coarse, exciting R&B sax-playing inflamed live audiences and outraged established musicians from the mid 1940s. Although his recording legacy included the comparatively mellow hit 'There Is Something On Your Mind', McNeely built up a huge audience with his frenetic live shows, whose appeal to both black and white audiences anticipated the advent of rock'n'roll. His legendary act culminated in antics such as the solo played while rocking on the stage on his back. Unsurprisingly, he retained his live following long after the hits dried up.

black audiences – and not a few young whites. At various times Bostic's band included saxophonists John Coltrane (1926-67), whom he tutored in producing high harmonics, and Stanley Turrentine (1934-), as well as pianist/organist Bill Doggett who would subsequently exert a profound influence on the course of jazz, soul and rock'n'roll with his hit 'Honky Tonk', an instrumental that combined Doggett's rippling organ with some punchy solos by Clifford Scott on tenor sax.

In the US during the 1940s and early 1950s the wealth of black music throughout the South and in the major urban areas refused to fit into simple niches. Most players making a living out of jump blues or R&B, for example, probably cut their teeth playing jazz. In straight blues, the tradition based on the legacy of early Delta players such as Charley Patton relied on straightforward guitar-based arrangements – yet singers like Bessie Smith and Ma Rainey had come to fame with horn-dominated ensembles. As time went on these two traditions fused in the person of guitarist T-Bone Walker, a pioneer of the newly-invented electric guitar.

Walker's first hit, 'T-Bone Blues', was recorded with Les Hite's big-band, but as he started to lead his own outfit he settled on a stripped-down big-band format with three or four horns that would become the standard for sophisticated blues – and, as we shall see, for soul.

But the advent of players such as Walker and jazzman Charlie Christian, who took the guitar out of the jazz rhythm section and made it respectable as a lead instrument, heralded a new, leaner era for horn players. The big-band format had doubtless emerged because many of the bandleaders – Count Basie and Duke Ellington included – needed an extended tonal range. Yet another part of the appeal was simply that a large number of musicians could provide the physical volume that was vital for dances in large auditoriums. But with the coming of amplification, a small band with a guitarist and four horns could drown out larger rivals. The economics were inescapable. As Rolling Stones guitarist Keith Richards later put it: "The electric guitar meant that you could have a band with a drummer and a couple of guitars. And that put a lot of horn players out of work."

ROCK AROUND THE CLOCK

It's a testament to the dominance of the saxophone that the record generally acknowledged as the first rock'n'roll recording – The Kings Of Rhythm's 'Rocket 88' – was credited to its sax player and vocalist, Jackie Brenston, rather than to bandleader Ike Turner. The formation of The Kings Of Rhythm was typical of many Memphis and Mississippi bands made up of musicians who'd worked in a wide variety of genres. Turner had played piano with bluesman Sonny Boy Williamson and even dabbled in country; Brenston, according to Ike Turner, was a fan both of jazz and of Louis Jordan-style jump blues, and had sat in with many Clarksdale and Memphis bands.

The vibrant Memphis musical scene boasted many small sax-led combos. But by this time the harmonica was already becoming a serious rival to the saxophone for one simple reason: despite the advent of budget US-made instruments, such as Buescher's Aristocrat line, the comparatively high price of the saxophone did put it beyond the reach of many aspiring musicians, some of whom doubtless turned to simpler, more affordable instruments.

Even if Jackie Brenston's lead credit on 'Rocket 88' was perhaps not completely justified, subsequent rock'n'roll records boasted plenty of saxophones. The best-known early rock'n'roll band, Bill Haley & His Comets, usually featured tenor saxophone as the lead instrument rather than guitar. One of their later songs, the instrumental 'Rudy's Rock', was even named after The Comets' saxophonist, Rudy Pompilli.

Haley and band were – if nothing else – adept at recognising the potential of sounds made by more original musicians, and turned R&B classics such as Brenston's 'Rocket 88' and Big Joe Turner's 'Shake Rattle & Roll' into pop hits. Haley's use of producer Milt Gabler emphasised his connection with Louis Jordan (Gabler had produced many of Jordan's biggest hits), and while Gabler himself claimed that there was no outright attempt to copy Jordan's sound, he did admit to humming Jordan's lines to Haley's musicians when working out arrangements. As far as Jordan was concerned, Haley's music represented a barely-competent copy of the sound he'd created. Nevertheless the raw energy and novelty of Haley's records ensured that they were huge sellers.

Black teenagers, meanwhile, were still buying records by sophisticated performers such as pianist/vocalists Amos Milburn or Percy Mayfield who were recording what was essentially stripped-down big-band music with an R&B edge.

Conn 10-M tenor saxophone
*c1959 (above) A typical saxophone of
the type used by rock'n'roll players in
the early- and mid-1950s. By this time,
however, the Conn company had hit
difficult times. The advertisement (left)
is for the Connstellation trombone,
introduced in 1955, a bright spot in a
decade marked by struggle and strife.*

King Super-20 tenor saxophone
*c1958 (right) Introduced immediately
after the war, the Super-20 was an
established favourite by the 1950s,
with its silver neck and bell and pearl-
inlaid keys. The advertisement (top)
lists "Some reasons why King Super
20s play better".*

Martin Magna baritone *saxophone c1948 (right) The baritone is the lowest-pitched member of the saxophone family in regular use, although lower-pitched bass saxophones and even contra-bass saxophones do exist. The baritone turns up most often in saxophone sections, like those in the rock'n'roll outfits seen on this page, where it provides a deep bottom end to* the ensemble sound. American rockers would have been most likely to use saxophones made by Conn, Selmer, King, Martin or Buescher. Martin saxophones of this vintage were excellent instruments. The company was subsequently sold by the Martin family and then sold again, moving in the process from Elkhart, Indiana, to Kenosha, Wisconsin.

This Martin advertisement *(below) was intended to dramatise the vast range of the company's interests, of which jazz was only a small part.*

Alvin 'Red' Tyler *(above) plays baritone, accompanied by an unidentified member of Big Joe Turner's band. Red Tyler was best-known for his New Orleans rock'n'roll sessions on baritone. His recording credits included Turner, Little Richard, Fats Domino, Art Neville, Earl King and most of the Crescent City's greats. After the rock'n'roll boom went to bust, Tyler returned to his first love, playing jazz on the tenor. He remained a much-loved regular at the New Orleans Jazz & Heritage Festival up until his death in early 1998.*

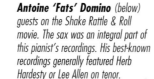

Antoine 'Fats' Domino *(below) guests on the Shake Rattle & Roll movie. The sax was an integral part of this pianist's recordings. His best-known recordings generally featured Herb Hardesty or Lee Allen on tenor.*

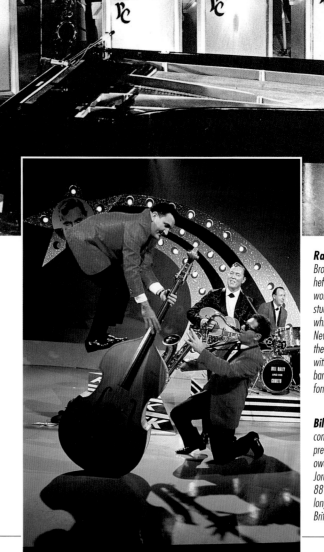

Ray Charles & big band *(above) Brother Ray's recipe for soul included a hefty portion of horns, a legacy of his work as an arranger in the New Orleans studios. Charles's first major band, which included David 'Fathead' Newman on tenor, was recruited from the cohorts of bluesman Lowell Fulson, with whom Charles played piano. Later bands used more jazzmen, including former Ellington and Basie players.*

Bill Haley's Comets *(left) The commercial breakthrough of Bill Haley, previously a Western swing musician, owed much to saxophonists Louis Jordan and Jackie Brenston, of 'Rocket 88' fame. Here Rudy Pompilli, Haley's long-term sax player, takes a solo on a British TV appearance.*

76

Selmer Mark VI alto *saxophone c1960 (left) Introduced in 1954, the Mark VI, prized for its ergonomic excellence, arrived just in time for rock'n'roll.*

79

Little Richard *used the cream of New Orleans' musicians. Early hits including 'The Girl Can't Help It' (right) used sessionmen Red Tyler on baritone and Lee Allen on tenor; later band members included Grady Gaines on tenor and Samuel Parker on baritone. For the 1960s British date shown above, Barry Cameron makes a guest appearance on baritone.*

King Curtis (left). Curtis Ousley became rock'n'roll's most celebrated saxophonist through such work as his instantly recognisable solo on The Coasters' 1958 hit 'Yakety Yak' Prompted to take up the sax by Louis Jordan ("I didn't know what it was he was playing, but I knew I wanted to play it"), Curtis worked with Lionel Hampton, then did sessions with Buddy Holly, The Drifters, Bobby Darin and others in the 1950s before scoring hits under his own name. When rock'n'roll faded out, Curtis's career continued. 'Soul Twist' of 1962 showed him ushering in a new era which continued with 1967's 'Soul Stew', recorded with Chips Moman's American Studios house band, the new sound in Memphis funk. As music changed, King Curtis changed too. He recorded major sessions with Sam Cooke, The Isley Brothers, Solomon Burke, Aretha Franklin, Wilson Pickett, as well as white rockers such as Eric Clapton and John Lennon. In the meantime, he recorded fine albums under his own name, such as 'Trouble In Mind', on which he also took a vocal role, and 'Party Time'. His career was still thriving when he was murdered outside his New York apartment in 1971.

One key figure in the recording of many such records was saxophonist Maxwell Davis (1916-70) who headed one of the leading studio bands on the West Coast, with a horn section that included Richard Wells on tenor saxophone and Charles Wallender on baritone. Davis's band was one of the most in-demand studio outfits in the US. As well as recording jukebox hits under its own name, Maxwell and crew were even given their own billing on recordings such as Davis's collaborations with B.B. King when the great blues guitarist opted for a touch of big-band sophistication.

WHEELIN' ON BOURBON

As rock'n'roll hit the pop charts in Haley's wake it took on a wide variety of forms, with its new performers drawn from country, blues and R&B backgrounds. But when record companies such as Specialty, Ace and Modern were looking for a reliable environment in which to record their artists, they knew there was one city they could rely on: New Orleans.

The cradle of jazz, New Orleans also boasted most of the best rock'n'roll performers in the country. The city had key strengths in three instrumental categories. Pianists were at the fore thanks to their instrument's position as an entertainment fixture in the local brothels. Drums were inspired by the "second line" tradition (named after the second line formed by percussion-playing participants at "jazz" funerals) as well as innovative players such as Earl Palmer. And it was of course the city's jazz tradition which accounted for the huge numbers of local horn players – but the fact that so many of them were so good was a wonderful added bonus.

Two further factors that counted in favour of New Orleans were the cut-throat musical competition that existed in the city, and a thriving after-hours scene in the major local clubs, The Dewdrop and The Tijuana.

Both clubs featured local musicians every night, and when visiting musicians such as B.B. King or T-Bone Walker played local venues they were expected to show up at the Dewdrop or Tijuana for late-night jam sessions. Although most of the local musicians regarded themselves as jazz players, they realised that R&B and rock'n'roll offered more lucrative prospects. Leading rock'n'roll personalities such as Roy Brown, Big Joe Turner, Little Richard and Fats Domino could all rely on making up their live bands from the huge local pool of talent

that regularly came in for session work at the tiny, bustling studio run by Cosimo Matassa on Rampart Street. Where rock'n'roll records cut in Memphis or New York might rely on a wide spread of musicians drawn from different areas, the New Orleans session scene revolved around a small nucleus of players, often centred on trumpeter and arranger Dave Bartholomew (1940-) who ran his own big-band and provided arrangements for sessions, or other local talents such as pianists Allen Toussaint and Huey Smith. However, the skill of the local horn players was such that, in reality, minimal musical direction was needed.

According to Cosimo Matassa, who oversaw practically every single hit produced in the city, the composer or singer might enter the studio with just a basic beginning, middle and ending for their songs, but the musicians themselves would come up with a horn arrangement within minutes. Often these would rely on standardised riffs, with the horn section and rhythm section working around basic patterns, but even so an astonishing amount of quick thinking was necessary. Alternate takes recorded at Matassa's studio in 1952 by Guitar Slim tell a revealing tale today. Slim, aka Eddie Jones, was at the time perhaps the most legendary guitarist in the South, but would arrive in the studio with the sketchiest of ideas; between takes his horn section, led by alto saxophonist Gus Fontanette and Charles Burbank, would evolve new riffs, new rhythms, or come in on different beats.

While many of the fine performers recording in New Orleans such as Big Joe Turner or Roy Brown were working with material that was essentially similar to the R&B of the 1940s, both Fats Domino and Little Richard developed genuinely new formats in the rush to fill the new, manic demand for rock'n'roll. Neither artist was constrained to the conventionally simple 12-bar formats, and each boasted some marvellously concise arrangements.

Fats Domino's band were equally adept at rolling boogies or Caribbean-influenced lilts. Domino's piano was often found in the background driving the rhythm while the wonderfully fat tenor saxophone of Herb Hardesty would trade lead lines with Fats's vocals. Domino's original saxophone line-up included Joe Harris on alto, Hardesty and Clarence Hall on tenors, and Alvin "Red" Tyler on baritone. Lee Allen played tenor on later Domino records, although Hardesty would still be playing with

Domino in the 1960s, a vital constituent of his sound. Little Richard's records for Specialty were a similar, typically New Orleans fusion where the piano, drums and horns all made up a democratic but exhilarating mix. Drummer Earl Palmer was generally the effective leader of Richard's band on studio sessions: when instructed to speed up takes on 'Tutti Frutti' he reportedly wound up an imaginary ratchet on his leg, counted the band in, and ensured the final recording hit the desired duration to the second. The horn section, usually led by Lee Allen, would use "head" arrangements, worked out in the studio and usually hummed to his colleagues by Allen or pianist Huey Smith, but again the details could vary substantially from take to take.

To add to the improvised nature of proceedings Matassa's rudimentary recording desk had just four microphone inputs, meaning that the horn section couldn't be allocated their own microphone. Instead they would be picked up as "spill" on the vocal or drum mikes – and with the live straight-to-mono recording there was no opportunity to correct a mistake with a later overdub. So when Lee Allen came to take a solo he would grab the Altec microphone placed over Earl Palmer's snare drum on a boom stand, pull it up to his sax, play the solo, and then return the stand to its original position after his allocated eight or 16 bars. "It worked, because it lowered the mid-range [sound frequencies] from the snare; then at the end of the solo you hear the drums come up as you go back into the song," recalls studio boss Matassa. "So quite a few of those things were happy accidents."

There was one more happy accident in Matassa's New Orleans studio that had especially far-reaching consequences. The sessions for Guitar Slim, Specialty's best-selling artist of 1954, had represented the studio debut of a young arranger called Ray Charles, who'd previously been a fan of the smooth singing styles of Nat King Cole and Charles Brown. Like many Specialty artists, Guitar Slim boasted a strong gospel feel, and while his biggest hit, 'The Things I Used To Do', had a basic three-chord blues progression, its 24-bar construction in 6/8 time gave it a totally different feel to a conventional 12-bar blues – particularly when Slim came in on the wrong beat.

The fact that the guitar and horn licks were based on a natural rather than flattened third added to the song's sound, and one that again was quite distinct from Slim's blues roots.

According to Robert Catfrey, who played tenor saxophone with Slim, "This was in the period when Slim was up there, Ray Charles was at his low, and he was still trying to do a Charles Brown, really, hanging around the Dewdrop."

Called in to oversee the session, Ray Charles did a tremendous job, working out an arrangement and catching even the smallest errors in the backing musicians. Yet while Charles doubtless contributed to the success of the song, Slim's sound would also have a significant effect on Ray's own career. From that point on Charles would drop his Charles Brown-style material and instead adopted a distinctively impassioned, gospel-influenced style taken directly from Slim. It would become Ray Charles's recipe for soul.

Charles's education was furthered by a stint as pianist with laidback bluesman Lowell Fulson, who had a big hit with 'Reconsider Baby' in 1954. Fulson boasted that he was the only band member who couldn't write music, but he had a legendary horn section led by tenor saxophonist David "Fathead" Newman and much admired by B.B. King.

When Charles left the band he took Newman and the horns with him. They would make up a pioneering soul section, although Fulson was left in the lurch until he found a replacement in the form of ex-Bostic tenor saxophonist, Stanley Turrentine. Although the emergence of soul itself was by no means straightforward, in the case of Ray Charles at least there's no doubt that the formative ingredients included a Guitar Slim-like gospel fervour coupled with a New Orleans R&B-style horn section.

A SWINGIN' AFFAIR

In retrospect, the advent of rock'n'roll represented a new beginning. For those already enjoying hits, rock'n'roll performers were the barbarians at the gates. For rock'n'roll wiped out a culture that was perhaps at its very peak in the mid 1950s, a sophisticated popular music that unlocked the potential of the newly-invented vinyl LP, most notably with recordings such as Frank Sinatra's *In The Wee Small Hours* and *Songs For Swingin' Lovers*. This hugely influential pair of groundbreaking LPs was recorded in the space of 12 months, between early 1955 and the beginning of 1956.

Sinatra's early pop material had been relatively disposable, but with the advent of the vinyl microgroove LP he raised

Olds press advertisement

(below). This press ad from a late 1950s Downbeat features celebrated arranger Nelson Riddle and Olds endorsee George Roberts, who played bass trombone with Riddle, Stan Kenton, Gene Krupa and other celebrated bands. The Olds company was established in California by trombonist Frank Ernest Olds in 1908. Although its Recording trumpets won a good reputation, F.E.Olds & Son would always be best-known for its trombones. The company's factory is now based in Elkhart, Indiana.

82

Couesnon Monopole B flat

piccolo trumpet c1960 (right) This instrument played the high trumpet part on The Beatles' 'Penny Lane'. Paul McCartney had seen David Mason and the English Chamber Orchestra performing a Brandenburg concerto on TV in January 1967. Mason was called in to Abbey Road, where McCartney apparently sang the part he needed. His fee for the 'Penny Lane' session was £27.50 (about $45). He did better in 1987 when the instrument was sold at Sotheby's for £6,380.

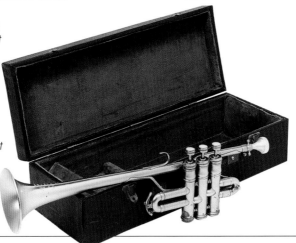

Long-playing Sinatra (above).

Sinatra recorded his first 12" long player, 'In The Wee Small Hours', in 1955. The album revitalised Sinatra's stalled career, demonstrated the potential of the new LP format, and helped establish an enduring relationship with the great arranger Nelson Riddle. Riddle, previously best-known for his work with Nat 'King' Cole, would collaborate on many classic Sinatra LPs for Capitol, including 'Songs For Swinging Lovers'. Other noted Sinatra arrangers included Billy May and Axel Stordahl.

Frank Sinatra (left) in action.
Sinatra was regarded as 'a prince' by
many of the musicians who worked
with him. His insistence on spontaneity
spills over to the grooves of his most
successful LPs.

Junior Walker (above) enjoyed a
string of mainly instrumental hits on
Motown subsidiary Soul from 1965.
Alto saxophonist and singer Walker
updated 1940s good-time jump blues
for the soul era, and with hits like
'Shotgun', and 'Roadrunner', Walker
and his All Stars were among
Motown's most successful chart acts
of the late 1960s.

Otis Redding on stage (above)
Redding and his Memphis backing
band, the Mar-Keys, shown here on tour
in England, helped establish the
Southern soul horn sound. Although the
Mar-Keys would later be devastated by
the plane crash that killed Redding in
December 1967, saxophonist Andrew
Love and trumpeter Wayne Jackson
would later work with Lou Reed, Robert
Cray and others as The Memphis Horns.

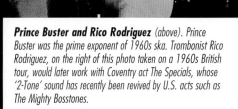

Prince Buster and Rico Rodriguez (above). Prince
Buster was the prime exponent of 1960s ska. Trombonist Rico
Rodriguez, on the right of this photo taken on a 1960s British
tour, would later work with Coventry act The Specials, whose
'2-Tone' sound has recently been revived by U.S. acts such as
The Mighty Bosstones.

The Skatellites (left). Early Jamaican ska was based around
a small nucleus of musicians including Rico Rodriguez and
Tommy McCook. McCook would later form The Skatellites, who
are still recording today.

popular music to a sophisticated art form – and it was an art form performed almost entirely on wind instruments. Sinatra's partner in the enterprise was arranger Nelson Riddle, who'd first come to the singer's attention with his work for Nat King Cole at Capitol. Riddle's first outing with Sinatra was in the style of established arranger Billy May, with whom the singer had worked previously.

Over subsequent years Riddle would arrange a sequence of albums that represents probably the most sophisticated horn-based popular music ever made (when Sinatra wanted slushy, string-based music he'd generally opt for another arranger, such as Gordon Jenkins). Riddle's orchestras were inevitably composed of jazzmen, and much of the material dated back to show-tunes of the 1930s and 1940s. But this was pop rather than jazz music. Even so, Sinatra was hip as far as his players were concerned, while by now his audience had moved from bobbysoxers to an older and more sophisticated set.

Riddle's exuberant, brassy arrangements were economical – but exhiliratingly flashy when necessary. Bandleader Stan Kenton had a substantial influence on several breakthrough Sinatra/Riddle collaborations; the densely-packed, swooping trombones and trumpets were a Kenton trademark that Riddle employed to greatest effect on Sinatra's recordings such as 'I've Got You Under My Skin'. The core of Sinatra's recording band included trumpeters Tom Harrell (1946-) and Harry "Sweets" Edison (1915-), plus baritone saxist Per Goldschmidt and George Roberts on bass trombone.

Sinatra and the orchestra were recorded live. Riddle was known for delivering arrangements at the very last moment and musicians would often have to sight-read their way through his unconventional, complex scores. Within the confines of the piece, musicians were allowed personal input which helped the music reach unprecedented heights; almost literally so in the case of ex-Kenton trombonist Milt Bernhart (1926-) who recorded the astounding trombone solo on 'I've Got You Under My Skin' spontaneously – and standing on a box. Recalling what would undoubtedly become the high point of his career, Bernhart ruefully remembered his first sight of the score: "Then I see that the whole thing is in G-flat [with six flats!]," recalled Bernhart, "which wouldn't bother the singer, but for the instrumentalist wasn't easy."

Bernhart's misgivings about the difficulty of the piece gave a boost of nervous energy to his exhilarating solo. Only when the rest of the orchestra stood up to applaud the successful take did Sinatra, Riddle and Bernhart realise they'd come up with something special.

Later in his career Sinatra would work with many distinguished arrangers and orchestras – Count Basie, a young Quincy Jones, even groovy 1960s cat Neal Hefti – and create a template for sophisticated pop that still holds good today.

YAKETY SAX

By 1957 it was obvious that rock'n'roll was here to stay. Two of the movement's most distinguished sax players epitomised the new direction in which horn sections were heading.

Curtis Ousley became famous as King Curtis (1934-71), the man who contributed instantly-recognisable tenor saxophone to dozens of hit singles for the Atlantic label. Curtis first hit the New York music scene with jazz bandleader Lionel Hampton and began earning a reputation which won him session work with vocalists such as Nat King Cole, Big Joe Turner and Chuck Willis, as well as with Atlantic-label groups such as The Drifters and The Coasters.

The Coasters' 'Yakety-Yak' was a King Curtis tour de force and helped establish a reputation which resulted in a string of hits made under his own name. Curtis's 'Soul Twist' in 1962 even managed briefly to restore the saxophone's reputation over the guitar as the premier popular lead instrument.

At a time when rock'n'roll was becoming clichéd and formulaic, Curtis added a vital rhythmic dimension. Today we'd probably describe his work as funky, and perhaps for exactly that reason he enjoyed hits right into the mid 1960s, recording with the cream of soul musicians including singers Solomon Burke, Aretha Franklin and Sam Cooke. In 1971, with his career as successful as ever, he was murdered outside his New York apartment.

Tenor saxophonist Steve Douglas could be described as the white rockabilly counterpart to Curtis. Douglas played an essential part in the series of instrumental singles recorded by guitarist Duane Eddy, inspired by alto saxman Bill Justis (1927-82) who had a string of instrumental hits with Sun, starting in 1957 with 'Raunchy'.

Eddy describes Douglas as "maybe the most important part of our sound – I always thought his sax was just as important

84

as the guitar on our records". Yet Eddy's billing as a guitar hero – perhaps the first in rock'n'roll – underlined a fact that by 1960 was becoming inescapable: the guitar player was the foremost instrumentalist in rock'n'roll. As surf music reached its height around 1961 in the US, to be succeeded by an English Invasion which took its inspiration from Buddy Holly and Chuck Berry, horn players seemed in danger of being wiped off the airwaves.

New Orleans was not the only place where jazzmen depped (deputised) in other musical styles in order to make a living. In Kingston, Jamaica, a distinct and unique set of musical and social influences were about to result in another startling new musical development.

The key to the evolution of Jamaican R&B lay in two strait-laced, long-established institutions: Alpha Boys School, and the Kingston Military School. Alpha Boys School was an old-fashioned Catholic school where parents sent their children for a formal and quite traditional education. Alpha had a strong musical tradition – and many of the students soon discovered that taking up the trumpet or trombone would get them out of other school chores.

Jamaica enjoyed a strong marching-band tradition, and the existing popularity of wind instruments together with the influences of those two schools would produce every major Jamaican horn player of the 1950s and early 1960s, including trombonists Rico Rodriguez (1934-) and Don Drummond (1943-), saxophonists Tommy McCook (1932-), Stanley "Ribs" Notice and Roland Alphonso (1936-), and trumpeters Lester Sterling, Johnny Moore and Baba Brooks. By 1950 tourism became a major Jamaican industry and there was a huge demand for horn players to work in the Harry James- or Duke Ellington-style big-bands run there by Eric Dean and Val Bennett. Rodriguez and his colleagues, formally trained and expert sight-readers, obliged.

Early in the 1950s an indigenous Jamaican music industry was stimulated by sound system owners (and forces of nature) such as Prince Buster, Coxsone Dodd and Duke Reid. The record labels for all the groundbreaking ska records of the late 1950s boasted exclusive-sounding names: Reid's crew were called the Duke Reid group, Coxsone worked with The Blues Blasters, and Prince Buster had his All Stars. In fact, all the bands boasted the very same horn section drawn from Rodriguez and his colleagues (plus Ernest Ranglin on guitar, Cluett Jonson on bass, and Arkland Parkes on drums). The horn players' monopoly subsequently continued – legendary ska outfit The Skatellites was formed by tenor man Tommy McCook around 1963 after Rodriguez had left the operation.

Rock steady, a more laidback, vocal-led music, succeeded ska, and the horn sections encountered a temporary slow-down. Yet as reggae established itself in Jamaica these same hornmen once more enjoyed a regular supply of studio work, aided by a new generation of sax and brass players who had been inspired by their example.

SOUNDS ORCHESTRAL

When The Beatles cut a swathe through American popular music, pop pundits in the US were either impressed by the Fab Four's freshness and energy or else horrified by the raw, primitive nature of their arrangements and recordings. By this point American producers and arrangers such as Leiber & Stoller, or Phil Spector and Jack Nitzsche, had developed ways of making records that went far beyond the basic instrumentation of rock'n'roll.

Jerry Leiber and Mike Stoller had started writing for artists like vocalists Jimmy Witherspoon and Charles Brown in Los Angeles. Ahmet Ertegun and Jerry Wexler subsequently bought Leiber & Stoller's fledgling label and recruited them as house producers for Atlantic Records in New York. Their earlier recordings were simple, using a rhythm section augmented by piano, guitar and King Curtis's sax. By 1963, when Atlantic had bought its first eight-track recorder years ahead of most of its rivals, Leiber & Stoller were using a substantial horn section with as many as 16 horn and wind players packed into their New York studio.

Phil Spector had collaborated with Leiber & Stoller on Ben E. King's 'Spanish Harlem', and from 1961 he tried to out-do their symphonic pop. Two key figures in his efforts were arranger Jack Nitzsche and Duane Eddy's tenor player Steve Douglas, now a regular in Spector's ace studio band The Wrecking Crew. Nitzsche epitomised the traditional role of arranger. "It's a vanishing art," he says now. "Back then the producer functioned more like a film producer, and the arranger was like the director."

Saxophonist Douglas took on an even greater responsibility

Fred Wesley (below) brought his trombone skills to James Brown's horn section, joining in time for 1968's 'Say It Loud - I'm Black and I'm Proud'. Starting in 1959 as a basic three-piece unit, the section grew and grew during

the 1960s. Wesley was one of those who left Brown's outfit in the mid-1970s to join George Clinton's Parliament/Funkadelic operation. James Brown's albums (below) continued to give prominence to his brass sections.

Maceo Parker (right) Parker is probably the best-known of James Brown's stellar saxophone lieutenants; he joined Brown in 1964, just in time to record 'Papa's Got A Brand New Bag.' Initially recruited on baritone, by the late 1960s Parker had switched to the tenor role. Subsequently acknowledged as leader of the JBs, Parker joined the Brown diaspora to Funkadelic, and recorded a series of LPs both as the JBs, and under his own name, which have lately proved a treasure trove for samplers.

Clarence Clemons and Bruce Springsteen (below) E-Street Band saxophonist Clarence Clemons, aka 'The Big Man', was Bruce Springsteen's foremost musical and visual foil. Clemons remained in-demand for

session work throughout the band's career, recording with Joan Armatrading and Carlene Carter, as well as recording a hit single with Jackson Browne. Since the dissolution of the E-Street Band in 1989, Clemons has led his own band, written movie soundtracks, and established an acting career.

Earth Wind and Fire (above) Formed in 1969 by vocalist Maurice White, Earth Wind and Fire achieved their first horn-driven hit with 1975's single 'Shining Star'. It was the first of a series of successes that continued into the 1980s. Tenor saxophonist Andrew Woolfolk (left in pic) joined in 1973, taking over leadership of the band's four-piece Phenix Horns section.

87

Yamaha YAS-62 alto saxophone c1996 (left) Modern saxophone companies offer a wide range of new instruments to budding saxophone players. The Japanese companies, such as Yamaha and Yanagisawa (whose advertisements are shown above), now rival some of the traditional French and American makers with fine instruments such as this example from Yamaha's easy-blowing YS series, first produced in 1980. Yanagisawa produced bugles at the turn of the century, building its first saxophone in 1954. Yamaha, in contrast, only entered the wind market in 1965 but within 10 years it was claiming to operate the largest wind instrument factory in the world.

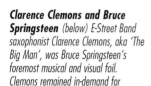

when during the 1960s The Wrecking Crew were recruited to play for one of Spector's greatest fans, Brian Wilson of The Beach Boys. The musicianship that Wilson began to demand from The Wrecking Crew increased in complexity over the years, reaching its apogee on 'Good Vibrations' and the *Pet Sounds* project. Steve Douglas was responsible for turning Wilson's hummed tunes into sometimes frighteningly complex arrangements. Plas Johnson (1931-), whose tenor saxophone can be heard on Henry Mancini's *Pink Panther* theme, Larry Williams's 'Bony Maronie', and The Coasters' 'Youngblood', was just one distinguished name in a talent-packed crew practically resident at LA's famed Gold Star studios for these innovative Beach Boys sessions.

It was without doubt the influence of *Pet Sounds* that spurred on The Beatles to similarly symphonic heights. The Liverpudlian group had started experimenting with more complex instrumentation after producer George Martin had worked out a spectacularly successful string-quartet arrangement for Paul McCartney's 'Yesterday'. By 1966 McCartney and Martin were calling in orchestral player Alan Civil to contribute the impeccable French horn obligato on 'For No One', and the roster of outside session musicians used on Beatles recordings began to increase over the next few years, primarily on McCartney songs.

After seeing piccolo-trumpet player David Mason on a TV performance of a Bach *Brandenburg Concerto*, McCartney suggested using him for the closing section of his latest work, 'Penny Lane'. Intent upon obtaining full value for Mason's session fee, McCartney asked George Martin, "What's the top note on that instrument?" The Beatle then insisted that Mason go a couple of notes higher. "David cursed me for years afterwards," McCartney recalls fondly.

MEMPHIS SOUL STEW

Although the British invasion moved the spotlight from saxophones to guitars, R&B music was constantly evolving and the horn section was still an integral part of its sound. King Curtis, who'd contributed tenor sax to so many great rock'n'roll records, found a new niche in many pioneering soul sessions.

Over that time the sound and image of soul saxophone changed profoundly, In 1963 Curtis was presenting urbane backing for the likes of Ben E. King with The King Curtis

Orchestra. By 1967 he would be working in Memphis, opting for a sweaty, downhome feel with the American House Band on pieces such as his 'Memphis Soul Stew' (named after the day's special that Curtis had spotted on the menu of Memphis's Ranch House Restaurant).

A key point in the history of soul music came when schoolboy Charles "Packy" Axton (1941-) convinced his guitar-playing schoolfriend Steve Cropper that Cropper's embryonic band The Royal Spades was in dire need of a horn section. Eventually, the consequent R&B band's name changed to The Mar-Keys, and by 1961 they had scored a pop hit with 'Last Night'. Tenor saxophonist Packy's mother was Estelle Axton, founder of the legendary Stax record label, and once the label recruited one-time gospel singer Otis Redding, soul music was in for an exciting ride.

"We did define that Southern soul horn style, but we didn't know what we were doing," says Mar-Keys trumpeter Wayne Jackson. "We weren't even experimenting, we were just playing what we could. Simple stuff. Otis had all the songs in his head when he came into the studio; the horn lines, bassline, guitar, everything," he says. Redding worked with a horn section that included Wayne Jackson, tenor saxophonist Andrew Love, and trumpeter Gene "Bowlegs" Miller. They would later work with artists such as Robert Cray under the Memphis Horns name.

Keyboard player Isaac Hayes describes how they would work with Redding: "Otis would get hold of the guitar and start running the groove down, and everybody would kinda catch on to what he was doin'," he says. "And eventually we would have a groove goin'. Then he'd have the horns come on, Wayne and Andrew and Gene – 'Daddle-daddle-daddle-dah-duh-laa!' – running the horn lines down to 'em till they started workin' on that. And the next thing you know, we'd pretty much have the arrangement in hand."

After Stax had established the stripped-down, funky basis of the Southern soul style, other studio bands emerged. Muscle Shoals soon became another source of soul hits when Atlantic started using the studio in the wake of Percy Sledge's hit, 'When A Man Loves A Woman'. According to engineer Jimmy Johnson the initial version of the song, recorded with three local horn players, was regarded as unusable by Atlantic's Jerry Wexler. "Jerry loved the song, but wanted us to re-cut it because the horns were so out of tune. So we brought Gene 'Bowlegs' Miller and a couple of other really good horn players down from Memphis, changed a couple of the background vocalists, re-did it, and sent it back. Well, whoever was mastering the record grabbed the original out-of-tune version, and that's the one that came out. When the record went to number one, Jerry Wexler called [Muscle Shoals boss] Quin Ivy and said, 'Baby, aren't you glad you re-cut that?' That was when Quin told him, 'Jerry, you used the *original* track.'"

Several of funk's greatest horn sections evolved directly from the amazing work of Little Richard's saxophonists Lee Allen and Red Tyler. James Brown was making a living impersonating Little Richard when he rewrote an old blues standard, 'Baby Please Don't Go', and came up with 'Please Please Please'. In 1957 Richard, newly converted to religion, cancelled a set of tour dates; Brown toured in his place and recruited a couple of Richard's Upsetters group, including saxophone players Lee Diamond and John White. In 1959 Brown recruited tenor saxophonist J.C. Davis as bandleader, and Davis headed a five-piece horn section up to 1961.

When Brown started out, his sound revealed the clear influences of Ray Charles and Little Richard. But it evolved quickly. By 1963's *Live At The Apollo* LP, with St Clair Pinckney heading the saxophone section, he'd become a major force in soul music. The following year, Brown was attempting to recruit the sensational young drummer Melvin Parker into his band. Melvin said he'd only join if Brown could make a place for his elder brother, Maceo.

Maceo Parker (1943-) played baritone saxophone for his early recordings with Brown, including the epochal 'Papa's Got A Brand New Bag'. The definitive 1965 recording of this song used a nine-piece horn section but was devastatingly concise, Parker's baritone solos dedicated specifically to accentuating the rhythm. The recording session was squeezed in between a gruelling journey on the tour-bus and the evening's performance in Charlotte, South Carolina. Brown would work by simply dictating lines of phrases and then letting his musicians assemble a groove. It was a difficult, time-consuming business. "During those times it was hard to figure out what the boss was doing or thinking," remembers Maceo Parker. "Sometimes you might work half a night on one tune." Somehow, Parker and the band managed to turn Brown's grunts and hand signals into one of the biggest records of 1965.

Brown's next breakthrough was, according to legend, invented by Maceo one afternoon while he was wandering around a music store in Cincinnati. 'Cold Sweat' adopted the trademark Brown technique of going for "the one" – hitting the first beat of each alternate bar in unison, then flying off into dazzling rhythmic territory for the next seven beats. The result was far removed from the big-band R&B that most of Brown's horn section had started on. The arrival in the band of trombonist Fred Wesley – and his subsequent departure to join George Clinton's Parliament-Funkadelic organisation – was another major step forward for funk. Their example proved that horns could play a vital role in the most minimalist and rhythm-oriented of musics. And as the glory days of funk arrived towards the end of the 1960s, horn players came to enjoy a new golden age.

BOOGIE WONDERLAND

In 1968 Sly & The Family Stone's joyful call to arms, 'Dance To The Music', ushered in a new populist era for black music which again dominated the pop charts. The likes of Prince and funk-era Johnny Guitar Watson would follow in Sly's footsteps, winning both white and black audiences. It was saxophone player Jerry Martini (1943-) who provided the impetus to put the Family Stone together.

"I'd go to the radio station where Sly worked as a DJ and tell him that we really got to start a band," Martini remembers. "He thought that I was the funkiest white boy around on saxophone... and I was. All of my peers were into Dave Brubeck. I listened to Lee Allen, the sax player for Little Richard. That was the stuff that made me start playing."

By the early 1970s countless major bands were using substantial horn sections. The Ohio Players, who evolved from Wilson Pickett's backing band, were a huge commercial success. As with many of their funkster contemporaries they were led by a horn player, saxophonist Clarence "Satch" Satchell, with Ralph "Pee Wee" Middlebrooks and Mervin Pierce on trumpet. The Ohio Players' sound would also inspire The Commodores, The Bar-Kays, and Cameo's Larry Blackmon among others.

Earth Wind & Fire had one of the most influential brass section sounds of all time, characterised by repetitive semi-quaver (16th-note) riffs. Although the band had its own

Phenix Horns led by tenor saxophonist Andrew Woolfolk (1950-), the section on its records was augmented with other players including British trumpeter Derek Watkins. Arrangements on the band's classic *I Am* album of 1979 were by experienced trumpeter Jerry Hey.

The extremely popular jazz-funk band The Crusaders had many hits that heavily featured tenor saxophone player Wilton Felder (1940-) and trombonist Wayne Henderson (1939-). Kool And The Gang too were led by a saxophone player, Ronald "The Captain" Bell (1951-), with Spike Mickens on trumpet, while blues funksters War would enjoy hits well into the 1970s driven by the harmonica of Lee Oskar and the saxophone and flute of Charles Miller (1939-).

THE GREAT GIG IN THE SKY

For the average saxophone player involved in rock music the 1970s saw a modest revival in the instrument's fortunes, and this improved position has more or less endured ever since. The influence of brassy, funky outfits such as James Brown and Sly & The Family Stone pervaded rock music, but a number of the most innovative bands of the 1970s came to use saxophones in new, strictly rock'n'roll formats.

Iggy Pop's Stooges had come to the attention of the US public in 1969, but their second album, *Funhouse*, would be regarded as the highpoint of their career. Its distinctive sound was inspired by new member Steve Mackay (1949-) on his Selmer Mark VI tenor. Mackay had learned to play saxophone formally at school, and after dabbling in various R&B bands joined The Stooges early in 1970, adding a dark, taut, R&B edge to the band's monumental punk sound.

Soon after Mackay arrived, the band recorded *Funhouse* as a direct, no-frills re-creation of their live set. Mackay remembers the live recording adding a distinct edge to the process. He worked with The Stooges until September of 1970, a *Billboard* review crediting him as leader of the band doubtless precipitating his dismissal. The timing was fortunate; Mackay left just as the entire band succumbed to the temptations of heroin. He went on to play with Commander Cody & His Lost Planet Airmen, having helped create a unique concoction that would influence David Bowie, The Damned and countless UK punk bands of the late 1970s, as well as Roxy Music whose debut album in 1972 had Andy Mackay (no

relation, 1946-) playing oboe and saxophone, including a Grafton plastic alto from the 1950s. It was also around this time that another saxman played a key role in the manifesto recording of a new musical genre. In 1972 Pink Floyd were still finding their way after the departure of founder member Syd Barrett. Well into the recording of a concept album on death, madness and money they decided to augment their sound with other musicians. Key among these was saxophonist Dick Parry, an experienced R&B player who'd once been in a Cambridge blues band with Floyd guitarist David Gilmour. The band were working on 'Money' when Parry was asked to contribute a sax part, Gilmour reportedly giving him the confusing brief of "sounding like the sax man in the cartoon band who did the theme for the Pearl & Dean ad sequence in the cinema".

Parry subsequently became an integral part of the band's live act, but a clue to the earnings of a freelance musician – as opposed to those of a band member – is perhaps best indicated by Parry's later sale of his Selmer tenor in a Sotheby's pop memorabilia auction. Such has often been the lot of the sax player in recent times, called in to provide a crucial part of many records while remaining in the economic margin. Thus Raphael Ravenscroft, who played on Gerry Rafferty's huge 1978 hit 'Baker Street'; Wesley Magoogan, who contributed a gorgeous solo on Hazel O'Connor's 1981 UK Top-20 'Will You'; or Ronnie Ross (1933-91), whose memorable tenor sax break was a crucial part of Lou Reed's biggest hit, 'Walk On The Wild Side' from 1973. Such musicians are rarely credited, and see few long-term benefits from musical contributions that help to make songs into hits.

Fortunately, not all players have been so undervalued. Fine saxophonists such as Tom Scott (1948-), Grover Washington Jr (1943-) and Ernie Watts (1945-) have made successful albums under their own names while also guesting with other acts. Alto saxophonist David Sanborn (1945-) worked with Paul Butterfield before joining The Brecker Brothers Band in 1975, and while he's guested with Stevie Wonder, Steely Dan, David Bowie and many more, his solo albums have sold to sophisticated music fans. Tenor sax player Michael Brecker (1949-) and tenor/soprano man Branford Marsalis (1960-) have also dabbled successfully in the pop world while managing to retain their jazz credibility.

Marsalis embodies the New Orleans trend of skilled jazz

POP SAXOPHONE AND BRASS

musicians who turn to rock as an alternative employment. His father, pianist Ellis, has been involved in musical education schemes in the city for over two decades, and the New Orleans Centre For Creative Arts which he helped to set up has schooled the likes of Harry Connick Jr, as well as brothers Wynton and Branford Marsalis. It is to be hoped that such courses will help ensure a continuing supply of skilled horn players at a time when music education budgets are being squeezed in the US.

Ironically, the move to guitar-dominated back-to-basics punk rock in late 1970s Britain also encouraged a new generation of horn players. This was partly due to punk's allegiance to reggae and a resurgence of interest in early ska. Even hardcore punks such as X-Ray Spex were using saxophones as a permanent part of their line-up, while post-punk band The Psychedelic Furs' dense, complex sound boasted obvious similarities with early Roxy Music.

By 1980 a new generation of British bands – including UB40 from Birmingham, The Specials from Coventry and Madness from north London – were wielding honking saxophones as an integral part of their sound. Specials leader Jerry Dammers established his own label, 2-Tone, in 1979, devoted to the looks and visuals of early ska – once the hip musical choice for 1960s mods. The label helped kick-start what would later be termed the 2-Tone "movement", and just as a whole new wave of young enthusiasts were inspired to pick up electric guitars because of punk, so a new British generation was turned on to the saxophone.

Madness were a typical example. Founder member Lee "Kix" Thompson (1957-) had been playing sax for a matter of months when he formed his first ska combo in 1976. Chas Smash (1959-) joined the band on bass the following year, but as their sound evolved under the influence of Prince Buster's records, Smash switched to trumpet. Like the rest of their band, Thompson and Smash were to say the least quite limited at first in their instrumental abilities, but aided by producers Clive Langer and Alan Winstanley they improved rapidly, and by 1985 Madness had become a successful UK chart act.

While the 2-Tone revival revealed roots in 1960s Jamaica, one of the most successful sax-dominated sounds of the 1980s harked back to the R&B that had given birth to rock'n'roll, as well as recalling the Spector-influenced grandiosity that saw pop reach symphonic new heights. Clarence Clemons (1942-)

had studied saxophone at school and majored in music with a bunch of friends who became The Vibratones. After a chance encounter with Bruce Springsteen's band he gave up his day job – and ultimately his marriage – convinced of the promise of early songs such as 'Spirit In The Night'. Clemons was influenced by saxmen King Curtis and Junior Walker (1942-), and his tenor added both Spectoresque drama and R&B grunt to Springsteen's impassioned epics. While Springsteen's legendary E-Street band included fine musicians such as guitarist Nils Lofgren, it was Clemons who often occupied the foreground. When the E-Street band was dissolved in 1989 Clemons built up a thriving solo career with his Red Bank Rockers, as well as writing and playing on movie soundtracks.

If Clemons' saxophone occupied centre-stage in the 1980s, the guitar and grunge rock of the 1990s once again pushed other instrumentalists into the background. Yet as music has diversified and countless bands revisit the greatest work of everybody from The Beach Boys to James Brown, the horn player has shown a remarkable resilience.

SAMPLED OR REAL?

There has been a growing cult of orchestral pop influenced by the arrangements of Jack Nitzsche and Beach Boy Brian Wilson, spearheaded by the duo Cardinal whose trumpet man Eric Matthews (trained at San Fransisco Conservatory of Music) has since started a solo career. "What's wrong with trumpets?" Matthews asks. "I'd be quite happy if I never used a guitar on a record." No-frills horn players have emerged with Orange County's revival of the brassy 2-Tone sounds of the early 1980s. And that bastion of the sampled lick, dance music, has seen increasing incursions from real instruments as bands like Air explore the sound of tubas and trumpets.

Meanwhile, guitar-dominated rock has grudgingly embraced wind instruments. Veteran trombonist Rico Rodriguez worked in the 1980s with UK ska band The Specials and more recently plays regularly with the Oasis-approved UK guitar band Ocean Colour Scene. He's confident that sax and brass will continue to hold their place in pop. "Man, I'm grateful people call me in to play on things," he says. "But I think it's getting better these days. People have had their keyboards, an' all that, but now they know they need to hear the air vibrate. For real music, they need real horn players."

THE SAX & BRASS DIRECTORY

SAX & BRASS DIRECTORY

This reference section is designed to give you some background information on a number of the significant saxophone, trumpet, cornet and trombone makers and their various brandnames, both past and present.

We've tried to give a potted history for each major brand, compiled from both official and unofficial sources. Sometimes, if the company still exists, they have supplied us with details which we've tried to translate into a relatively factual account, bearing in mind that it is the natural inclination of some companies to exaggerate and over-play their role in the development of various instruments. Unofficial sources vary from deep academic studies to casual notes written by contemporary workers. Given all this, and despite Balafon's customary editorial zeal, there will be inaccuracies. If you see any that you know about, please contact the publisher. We are especially interested to hear from people who may have worked at the various companies, or from existing companies who suddenly realise that they should have a fuller story in future editions.

Serial number lists also come from a variety of sources (see the acknowledgements on page 120 for a list of our valued helpers, both historical and numerical). The companies themselves are often not willing to divulge serial numbers of more recent dates. Apparently they think that their rivals will seize upon this information and somehow turn it against them. That is why you will very often see here detailed information up to a relatively recent date... and then nothing. Once again, if you have corrections or updates on serial numbers, please contact the publisher. It should also be borne in mind that serial numbers *do not* provide absolute dating of a given instrument. Official lists may be "massaged" (upwards by large companies who want to appear to be making more than they do; downwards by smaller ones who want to appear as exclusive as possible). It's difficult to interpret from some records whether a date on a serial number list refers to an instrument made at the very end of that year, the middle of the year, or the beginning – so our lists have been printed here with a generous leeway where we're unsure (which is in most cases). Numbers may have been mis-recorded. Typists may have (understandably) dozed off during the mid 1920s. Things may have been made up. So date your horn with a large pinch of salt available. And play that thing, OK?

While despairing of some companies' flagrant disregard for their own histories – and some of them are surely selling history as much as they are selling musical instruments – we do have here what is, we firmly believe, the most complete set of histories and dating information for saxophones and brass instruments ever put into print. We hope it gives you many happy and useful hours of pleasure that equal our own in compiling it.

ADOLPHE

See SAX.

AMERICAN ARTIST

See BUESCHER.

AMERICAN STANDARD

See KING.

ARTIST

See BUESCHER.

VINCENT BACH

Vincent Bach was born Vincent Schrotenbach in Vienna, Austria, in 1890. The young Vincent was taught to play violin and bugle at first, but found that he preferred the trumpet and switched to that instrument at the age of 12. Despite graduating from the Maschinenbauschule (mechanical engineering college) with a degree in engineering, he decided on a musical career.

As a talented cornet player he toured throughout Europe, playing an instrument made by the German Alexander Brothers. It was while he was in England that he decided to change his name to Vincent Bach. Escaping detention there as an "enemy alien" in 1914 at the start of World War I, Bach fled to the United States, taking with him a Besson instrument. At first he worked in vaudeville theatres, but soon landed a job with the Boston Symphony Orchestra after writing to conductor Karl Mück. By 1915 Bach was first trumpet in the Dyagilev Ballet Orchestra at the Metropolitan Opera House in New York, and performed at the American premieres of Stravinsky's Petrushka and The Firebird.

While Bach was on tour in Pittsburgh a local repairman convinced him that his mouthpiece could be improved – but the result was a disaster. Bach became determined to provide a reliable mouthpiece service for brass-playing musicians, and began by setting up in the back of the Selmer music store in New York, refurbishing old mouthpieces as well as producing new ones.

In 1918 Bach spent $300 on a foot-operated lathe, and rented a room in New York opposite the Musicians' Union headquarters. During the day he developed his mouthpiece business there; at night, he performed at the Rivoli Theater. An ad in a music magazine reading "How to become a wizard on the cornet without practicing" pulled in $500-worth of orders in its first few weeks, and Bach never looked back. By 1922, now at East 41st Street, Bach had ten employees.

As a logical step from mouthpiece production Bach started to manufacture instruments. In 1924, a year after he became a US citizen, Bach produced his first trumpets and cornets, instituting the Stradivarius model name to stress quality. Later model names included Apollo, Mercedes (introduced 1950s), Mercury (1950s), Minerva (1958) and New Yorker. Four years later Bach moved to the Bronx in New York, and began making tenor and bass trombones. Despite the stock market crash and the Depression, Bach and his new instrument firm prospered, although business remained very sluggish during the 1940s when the factory was largely switched to undertaking repair work. In 1953 Bach moved its location from the Bronx to a new factory at Mount Vernon in New York state.

In 1961 Bach decided at the age of 71 to sell his company. Apparently 13 buyers expressed an interest, but despite higher offers among the rest, Bach chose to sell to Selmer, doubtless a sentimental decision recalling the roots of his business back in the Selmer store almost fifty years earlier. The sale was completed in 1961, and the Bach tooling and machinery was moved to Selmer's base in Elkhart, Indiana, where Bach instruments have been made since 1965. Vincent Bach died in 1976.

As well as cornets, trumpets and trombones, the Bach line today includes flugelhorns, single and double horns, and mellophones. The Music Trades magazine estimated recently that Bach instruments command well over 60 per cent of the high-end brass market in the US.

BACH SERIAL NUMBERS 1924-1994

Bach production is often considered as dividing into three geographically-related periods: "New York" 1924-1953; "Mount Vernon" 1953-1965; and "Elkhart" 1965 to date.

95

BACH SERIAL NUMBERS 1924-1994

Numbers listed in the left hand column of the chart below denote the approximate number range and the relevant production years are set in italic type on the right.

Trumpets and Cornets

Range	Years
001-500	1924-26
501-600	1926-27
601-900	1927-28
901-1,450	1928-30
1,451-2,250	1930-35
2,251-4,650	1935-40
4,651-5,500	1940-41
5,501-6,500	1941-45
6,501-9,100	1945-50
8,600-8,799 (1)	1928
9,101-12,000	1950-53
10,000-10,999 (2)	1939
12,001-13,600	1953-55
13,601-19,500	1955-60
19,501-21,000	1960-61
21,001-24,000	1961-64
24,001-30,000	1964-65
30,001-50,000	1965-70
50,001-100,000	1970-74
100,001-112,000	1974-75
112,001-175,000	1975-80
175,001-200,000	1980-81
200,001-230,000	1981-83
230,001-250,000	1983-85
250,001-336,000	1985-90
336,001-420,000	1990-94

Trombones

Range	Years
001-200	1928-33
201-400	1933-35
401-1,600	1935-40
1,601-2,200	1940-42
2,201-2,500	1942-45
2,501-3,450	1945-50
3,451-4,500	1950-55
4,501-5,700	1955-60
5,701-5,950	1960-61
5,951-6,900	1961-64
6,901-8,000	1964-65
8,001-11,800	1965-70
8,600-8,799 (1)	1928
10,000-10,999 (2)	1939
11,801-17,500	1970-75
17,501-25,000	1975-77
25,001-39,000	1977-79
39,001-45,000	1979-81
45,001-55,000	1981-83
55,001-65,000	1983-85
65,001-91,000	1985-90
91,001-115,000	1990-94

(1) Apollo   (2) Mercury

BENGE

The company was founded by Elden Benge who was first trumpeter with the Detroit and later the Chicago Symphony Orchestras. Benge decided that he could improve on the instruments available to him, and built the first Benge trumpet in the late 1930s. By 1952 his manufacturing operation was moved to Burbank in the Los Angeles area, and Elden's son Donald Benge took over on his father's death in 1960. In the early 1970s the Benge company was bought by King, who moved the factory to Anaheim, California. These Californian production locations made Benge especially popular with West-coast musicians in the 1960s and 1970s. Then in 1983, when King was bought by Bernhard Muskantor, Benge production was shifted to Eastlake, Ohio. Shortly afterwards Muskantor bought Armstrong flutes and Conn, and formed United Musical Instruments (UMI), under whose umbrella Benge trumpets, cornets and trombones continue in production today.

96

BENGE SERIAL NUMBERS

Trumpets and Cornets

Numbers listed in the left hand column of the chart below denote the approximate number range and the relevant production years are set in italic type on the right.

up to 10,000	to end of 1973
10,001-12,000	1973-74
12,001-14,000	1974-75
14,001-18,000	1975-76
18,001-21,000	1976-77
21,001-26,000	1977-78
26,001-30,000	1978-79
30,001-34,000	1979-80

BESSON

Besson was founded in Paris in the late 1830s by Gustave Auguste Besson, and by the 1840s Besson was manufacturing brass instruments, including cornets. In 1858 Besson set up new premises in London, having left Paris as a result of losing a legal battle with Adolphe Sax, the inventor of the instrument. The involvement in the business of Gustave's wife, Florentine, led to both Paris- and London-made Besson instruments being stamped "F. Besson" from the 1860s, the "F" standing for Florentine (some accounts suggest it stands for "Fontaine").

After Gustave's death in 1874 his widow and his daughter Marthe took over the business. Some of Besson's mid-19th century production developments, especially the use of prototype "mandrels" and their bore design, led to some now-standard modern brass manufacturing techniques and designs.

During the 1890s the Besson family sold the British company, after which London-made instruments were stamped "Besson & Co" (some were sold in the US through the Carl Fischer company). Besson continued to stamp their own Paris-made instruments with "F. Besson".

Besson were especially noted for cornets, and for special low- and high-pitch trumpets, including the first piccolo G trumpet (1880s). Besson's Meha Bb trumpet introduced in the 1930s was very influential on many modern makers. Besson was bought by Boosey & Hawkes in 1948.

BESSON PARIS SERIAL NUMBERS 1869 TO 1947

Numbers listed in the left hand column of the chart below denote the approximate number range and the relevant production years are set in italic type on the right.

001-10,000	1869-74
10,001-14,000	1874-76
14,001-24,143	1876-79
24,144-26,000	1879-82
26,001-30,000	1882-84
30,001-36,000	1884-87
36,001-40,000	1887-89
40,001-50,000	1889-94
50,001-68,000	1894-1901
68,001-69,000	1901-05
69,001-70,000	1905-06
70,001-77,500	1906-11
77,501-82,000	1911-20
82,001-87,000	1920-34
87,001-92,000	1934-47

BESSON LONDON SERIAL NUMBERS 1858 TO 1952

Brass and Saxophones

001-10,800	1858-1870
10,801-17,600	1870-75
17,601-28,815	1875-83
28,816-35,500	1883-86
35,501-35,835	1886-87
35,836-45,000	1887-90
45,001-52,000	1890-94
52,001-55,134	1894-95
55,135-63,000	1895-98
63,001-76,000	1898-1903
76,001-90,000	1903-09
90,001-93,000	1909-11
93,001-100,200	1911-14
100,201-101,500	1914-17
101,501-111,500	1917-21
111,501-124,350	1921-31
124,351-130,000	1931-34
130,001-135,000	1934-48
135,001-141,116	1948-52

Trombones only

up to 3,070	to end of 1905
3,071-9,000	1906-08
9,001-9,950	1908-12
9,951-10,800	1912-16
10,801-11,600	1916-19
11,601-12,600	1919-24
12,601-13,950	1924-35
13,951-14,659	1935-40
14,660-15,088	1940-50

BOOSEY & HAWKES

Boosey & Hawkes was founded in 1930 when two British companies – Boosey & Co and Hawkes & Son – were merged. John Boosey had founded a music lending library in

London in the 1760s, and his operation expanded rapidly into music publishing as he acquired rights to band and orchestral works. He formed Boosey & Co in 1816. In the 1850s Boosey began making brass and wind instruments, while continuing to develop his publishing interests. Boosey & Co established an office in New York in 1892.

Hawkes & Son was founded in 1865 by William Henry Hawkes, rivalling Boosey in its band and orchestral music publishing and, later, musical instrument production. Hawkes built an instrument factory in north London in 1925 that is still active for Boosey & Hawkes today.

The merger in 1930 created Boosey & Hawkes, significantly strengthening its combined international music publishing power. The old Hawkes brandname of 20th Century (sometimes shown as "XXth Century") which had been used in the 1920s for a line of saxophones was continued into the 1930s by Boosey & Hawkes, who also began to sell under their new combined brandname various saxophones and brass instruments drawn from several manufacturing sources.

Today Boosey & Hawkes manufacture a wide range of instruments, using various famous brass and wind brandnames acquired over the years such as F. Besson (bought in 1948), Buffet Crampon (1981) and Julius Keilwerth (1989). The Boosey & Hawkes brandname itself was discontinued around 1982, although the imported student lines are still branded "B&H 400".

BOOSEY & CO SERIAL NUMBERS TO 1934

Numbers listed in the left hand column of the chart below denote the approximate number range and the relevant production years are set in italic type on the right.

Brass

up to 36,932	*to end of 1891*
36,933-41,506	*1891-92*
41,507-43,393	*1892-93*
43,394-45,080	*1893-94*
45,081-46,572	*1894-95*
46,573-47,880	*1895-96*
47,881-49,539	*1896-97*
49,540-51,590	*1897-98*
51,591-53,895	*1898-99*
53,896-56,375	*1899-1900*
56,376-59,198	*1900-01*
59,199-61,677	*1901-02*
61,678-64,179	*1902-03*
64,180-66,495	*1903-04*
66,496-68,978	*1904-05*
68,979-71,718	*1905-06*
71,719-73,814	*1906-07*
73,815-75,600	*1907-08*
75,601-77,423	*1908-09*
77,424-79,257	*1909-10*
79,258-81,723	*1910-11*
81,724-83,688	*1911-12*
83,689-85,996	*1912-13*
85,997-88,523	*1913-14*
88,524-93,415	*1914-15*
93,416-98,316	*1915-16*
98,317-100,679	*1916-17*
100,680-103,990	*1917-18*
103,991-104,183	*1918-19*
104,184-108,455	*1919-20*
108,456-111,174	*1920-21*
111,175-114,261	*1921-22*
114,262-116,945	*1922-23*
116,946-119,411	*1923-24*
119,412-121,910	*1924-25*
121,911-125,285	*1925-26*
125,286-128,009	*1926-27*
128,010-131,460	*1927-28*
131,461-134,299	*1928-29*
134,300-136,685	*1929-30*
136,686-138,565	*1930-31*
138,566-140,164	*1931-32*
140,165-141,820	*1932-33*
141,821-145,643	*1933-34*

Reeds Including Saxophones

up to 10,948	*to end of 1891*
10,949-10,994	*1891-92*
10,995-11,436	*1892-93*
11,437-11,843	*1893-94*
11,844-12,163	*1894-95*
12,164-12,476	*1895-96*
12,477-12,797	*1896-97*
12,798-13,184	*1897-98*
13,185-13,452	*1898-99*
13,453-13,865	*1899-1900*
13,866-14,328	*1900-01*
14,329-14,793	*1901-02*
14,794-15,261	*1902-03*
15,262-15,682	*1903-04*
15,683-16,228	*1904-05*
16,229-16,678	*1905-06*
16,679-17,162	*1906-07*
17,163-17,600	*1907-08*
17,601-18,060	*1908-09*
18,061-18,497	*1909-10*
18,498-18,894	*1910-11*
18,895-19,437	*1911-12*
19,438-20,062	*1912-13*
20,063-20,425	*1913-14*
20,426-21,182	*1914-15*
21,183-21,605	*1915-16*
21,606-21,963	*1916-17*
21,964-22,192	*1917-18*
22,193-22,406	*1918-19*
22,407-22,918	*1919-20*
22,919-23,490	*1920-21*
23,491-24,064	*1921-22*
24,065-24,730	*1922-23*
24,731-25,144	*1923-24*
25,145-25,661	*1924-25*
25,662-26,172	*1925-26*
26,173-26,824	*1926-27*
26,825-27,339	*1927-28*
27,340-27,874	*1928-29*
27,875-28,696	*1929-30*
28,697-29,458	*1930-31*
29,459-29,809	*1931-32*
29,810-30,403	*1932-33*
30,404-30,981	*1933-34*

HAWKES & CO SERIAL NUMBERS 1914 TO 1930
Brass

up to 32,000	*to end of 1914*
32,001-39,000	*1914-15*
39,001-60,000	*1915-30*

BOOSEY & HAWKES SERIAL NUMBERS 1935 TO 1985

Numbers listed in the left hand column of the chart below denote the approximate number range and the relevant production years are set in italic type on the right.

Brass

up to 145,199	. .to end of 1935
145,200-146,673	1935-36
146,674-148,811	1936-37
148,812-151,140	1937-38
151,141-153,435	1938-39
153,436-155,743	1939-40
155,744-157,774	1940-41
157,775-159,290	1941-42
159,291-159,898	1942-43
159,899-160,568	1943-44
160,569-161,408	1944-45
161,409-162,913	1945-46
162,914-165,575	1946-47
165,576-169,451	1947-48
169,452-172,247	1948-49
172,248-174,903	1949-50
174,904-177,608	1950-51
177,609-180,519	1951-52
180,520-182,842	1952-53
182,843-185,201	1953-54
185,202-192,569	1954-55
192,570-211,560	1955-56
211,561-238,659	1956-57
238,669-269,345	1957-58
269,346-288,450	1958-59
288,451-303,448	1959-60

Reeds Including Saxophones

30,982-39,725	1935-45
39,726-46,450	1945-46
46,451-47,175	1946-47
47,176-50,900	1947-48
50,901-51,577	1948-49
51,578-52,254	1949-50
52,255-52,931	1950-51
52,932-68,605	1951-52
68,606-84,279	1952-53
84,280-99,953	1953-54
99,954-115,630	1954-55
115,631-129,184	1955-56
129,185-142,738	1956-57

New Series

up to 58,835	1957-58
58,836-59,144	1958-59
59,145-62,458	1959-60
62,459-65,957	1960-61
65,958-69,718	1961-62
69,719-75,320	1962-63
75,321-78,094	1963-64
78,095-93,206	1964-67
93,207-99,332	1967-68
99,333-105,618	1968-69
105,619-111,417	1969-70
111,418-117,748	1970-71
117,749-126,210	1971-72
126,211-133,904	1972-73
133,905-143,518	1973-74
143,519-153,324	1974-75
153,325-163,568	1975-76
163,569-173,827	1976-77
173,828-183,902	1977-78
183,903-191,873	1978-79
191,874-201,532	1979-80
201,533-210,653	1980-81
210,654-221,261	1981-82
221,262-234,696	1982-83
234,697-250,372	1983-84
250,373-266,397	1984-85

BUESCHER

In 1888 Gus Buescher left the Conn company and set up the Buescher Band Instrument Company, based like Conn in Elkhart, Indiana, and at first concentrating on trumpet production (although later ads claim the company as "supreme in saxophones since 1888"). A fire in 1905 restricted production for a while, but by the 1920s Buescher, along with its chief rival Conn, dominated the booming saxophone business in the US. Buescher's True Tone line of saxophones was made until about the mid 1930s (although the company continued to use "True Tone" as a sales motto for many years). Buescher was also an early champion of the C-melody saxophone, which was easier to play with piano music than standard-key saxophones.

Production of saxophones in the US reached a peak in 1924 when some 100,000 units were manufactured by the American brands, principally in Elkhart,

Indiana, the base for both Buescher and Conn. In the 1920s Buescher was owned by a syndicate that included Conn's boss Carl Greenleaf and the keyboard manufacturer Wurlitzer. "Stencil" instruments were especially prevalent in the US saxophone boom in the 1920s; the term indicates the manufacture of instruments by a major maker – including Buescher – stamped with a brandname to suit the customer. Thus Buescher built saxophones and brass instruments bearing the names of American Artist, Artist, Carl Fischer, Lyon & Healy, Selmer (US) or Wurlitzer, among others. Buescher also made their own cheaper line with the Elkhart brand.

Later Buescher-brand saxophone models included the popular Aristocrat (introduced around 1933) and the professional 400 (introduced around 1942). Carl Greenleaf's son Charles left Conn in the late 1950s to head Buescher, but sold Buescher to Selmer US in February 1963. Selmer US continued the Buescher

name for a while, basing the instruments on existing tooling but cheapening them by using poorer materials, and these saxophones are not well regarded. Selmer eventually absorbed some Buescher elements into their cheaper Bundy and Signet student lines.

BUESCHER/BUNDY SERIAL NUMBERS TO 1983

Numbers listed in the left hand column of the chart below denote the approximate number range and the relevant production years are set in italic type on the right.

Saxophones

up to 5,000	. . . . .to end of 1905
5,001-11,250	1905-10
11,251-25,103	1910-15
25,104-61,255	1915-20
61,256-175,275	1920-25
175,276-255,250	1925-30
255,251-269,000	1930-35
269,001-291,000	1935-40
291,001-303,000	1940-45
303,001-332,000	1945-50
332,001-350,000	1950-55
350,001-360,000	1955-60
360,001-381,000	1960-63
381,001-408,818	1963-65
408,819-520,000	1965-70
520,001-630,000	1970-75
630,001-785,000	1975-80
785,001-875,000	1980-83

BUFFET CRAMPON

The Buffet Crampon company dates back to 1825 when Buffet Auger established a woodwind manufacturing business in France. Leon Crampon became a partner in 1871. In 1850 the company built a factory in Mantes, outside Paris, primarily for clarinet manufacture (it is still active today).

In the 1880s the company's owner, Pierre Goumas, sold Buffet Crampon to Paul Evette and Ernest Schaeffer. Goumas had already developed the saxophone in France with some useful modifications to Adolphe Sax's keywork, and produced a number of well-made instruments. Evette & Schaeffer too made some fine saxophones, continuing to produce them into the 1930s (some were also made with Buffet Crampon markings) and including one of the few commercially available contra-bass models.

These pioneering French manufacturers – Goumas, Evette-Schaeffer and Buffet Crampon – were among the leading makers of early saxophones. Later, some less noteworthy Buffet Crampon saxophones were made, including

the Dynaction model of the 1950s and 1960s. Buffet Crampon was acquired by Boosey & Hawkes in 1981 and continues to make clarinets, which are still highly regarded.

BUNDY

See BUESCHER and SELMER (PARIS).

CALICCHIO

Dominick Calicchio was born in Rome in 1901 and although he was not a musician he soon began working on brass instruments, beginning at the age of ten. He emigrated from Italy to the US in the 1920s and began making mouthpieces at the Rudy Mück brass factory in New York. Having become an accomplished tool-and-die maker and craftsman, Calicchio left Mück in 1927 to design and build his own trumpets and mouthpieces, and soon moved to California.

Calicchio's innovations resulted in two US patents, for an adjustable cup (1948) and a component mouthpiece kit (1976). During his working life he built a

CALICCHIO SERIAL NUMBERS 1927-1998

Numbers listed in the left hand column of the chart below denote the approximate number range and the relevant production years are set in italic type on the right.

1000-1300	*1927-1947*
1301-2800	*1947-1979*
2801-6000	*1979-1998*

Calicchio serial number notes
Some earlier casings were stamped with a number but not used, so in fact fewer than the implied 1800 instruments were made in the 1927-1979 period. Of the recent total for 1979-1998 about 25 were Williams trombones. Current production averages 200 trumpets per year.

little less than two thousand trumpets. Calicchio died in 1979, since when his daughter Irma Calicchio has continued the business, and Dominick's grandson, Christopher Calicchio Weik, who began working in his grandfather's workshop after school, maintains the instrument company. The Calicchio operation has also produced Williams trombones since purchasing that company in 1994.

CLEVELAND

See KING.

99

BUFFET CRAMPON SERIAL NUMBERS TO 1985

Numbers listed in the left hand column of the chart below denote the approximate number range and the relevant production years are set in italic type on the right.

Saxophones

up to 2,925	*to end of 1952*	4,818-5,392	*1957-58*
2,926-3,115	*1952-53*	5,393-6,172	*1958-59*
3,116-3,390	*1953-54*	6,173-6,808	*1959-60*
3,391-3,763	*1954-55*	6,809-7,416	*1960-61*
3,764-4,226	*1955-56*	7,417-8,656	*1961-62*
4,227-4,817	*1956-57*	8,657-9,669	*1962-63*
		9,670-10,064	*1963-64*
		10,065-11,749	*1964-65*
		11,750-12,778	*1965-66*
		12,779-13,776	*1966-67*
		13,777-14,487	*1967-68*
		14,488-15,347	*1968-69*
		15,348-16,323	*1969-70*
		16,324-17,319	*1970-71*
17,320-18,455	*1971-72*		
18,456-19,787	*1972-73*		
19,788-21,441	*1973-74*		
21,442-22,687	*1974-75*		
22,688-24,417	*1975-76*		
24,418-26,151	*1976-77*		
26,152-27,280	*1977-78*		
27,281-28,733	*1978-79*		
28,734-30,190	*1979-80*		
30,191-31,539	*1980-81*		
31,540-32,961	*1981-82*		
32,962-33,924	*1982-83*		
33,925-34,664	*1983-84*		
34,665-35,733	*1984-85*		

CONN

Charles Gerard Conn was born in upstate New York in 1844. As a 21-year-old Civil War veteran, Conn invented a brass mouthpiece in 1874 for which patents were soon granted. The story goes that Conn devised his original mouthpiece after suffering a split lip in a bar brawl and, wanting to continue to play cornet in a local band, came up with a rubber-rimmed mouthpiece ("a cushion for the lips," Conn called it) that enabled him to play comfortably.

Having developed a process to vulcanise rubber to metal, Conn soon started manufacturing his mouthpieces, at first in humble premises over a drugstore in Elkhart, Indiana. In 1876, convinced that he needed specialist help, Conn persuaded a skilled French instrument maker, Eugene Dupont, to leave his employ at the Distin company in England and bring with him a small team of craftsmen. They subsequently formed the Conn-Dupont company, and started production of the Conn Four-In-One cornet, playable in four different keys. The Conn-Dupont operation lasted until 1879 when Conn regained full control of his company.

It was in effect these early events that would lead to Elkhart becoming the brass and wind instrument capital of America, a position that it still holds today (the city produced some 60 per cent of all the wind instruments sold in the US in 1997).

Back in 1883 the Conn factory suffered a major fire, burning the building to the ground, but the city of Elkhart provided a large loan to help Conn back into business; Conn had been voted the city's first Democrat mayor three years earlier. Conn introduced the Wonder line of models at this time, and endorsers would include the famous wind bandleader John Philip Sousa, whose band was at one time kitted out with a complete set of gold-plated Conns. Sousa later worked with Conn to design the sousaphone. Soon Conn claimed the largest factory of its kind in the world, employing some 300 workers (many of whom were brought to Elkhart from France and England). In 1886 Conn opened a second plant at Worcester, Massachusetts, in the former Fiske instrument factory; this lasted until 1898.

In 1888 Conn made the first US-built saxophone, designed by Eduard A. Lefébre, and added saxophone models to its Wonder line, including soprano, alto, tenor and baritone. Born in 1834 in France, Lefébre was a clarinet virtuoso in his native country before his 20th birthday, and upon meeting Adolphe Sax fell in love with the saxophone and soon became a virtuoso on that instrument as well. Moving to the US in the 1850s, Lefébre joined Patrick Gilmore's famous 22nd

100

CONN SERIAL NUMBERS

Numbers listed in the left hand column of the chart below denote the approximate number range and the relevant production years are set in italic type on the right.

Reeds Including Saxophones

up to 2,000 . . . .to end of 1896	21,201-22,500 1911-12	278,001-284,000 1937-38	A, B or C plus five digits .1962-4
2,001-2,500 1896-97	22,501-25,000 1912-13	284,001-285,000 1938-39	D or E plus five digits . . .1964-5
2,501-3,000 1897-98	25,001-30,000 1913-15	285,001-288,300 1939-40	F, G or H plus five digits .1965-6
3,001-3,500 1898-99	30,001-35,000 1915-16	288,301-295,250 1940-41	J or K plus five digits 1966-7
3,501-3,900 1899-1900	35,001-40,000 1916-18	295,251-304,500 1941-42	K or L plus five digits . . .1967-8
3,901-4,400 1900-01	40,001-50,000 1918-19	304,501-309,250 1942-43	M plus five digits* 1968-9
4,401-5,100 1901-02	50,001-58,000 1919-20	309,251-309,300 1943-44	N plus five digits 1969-0
5,101-6,700 1902-03	58,001-64,000 1920-21	309,301-310,200 1944-45	P plus five digits 1970-1
6,701-8,500 1903-04	64,001-83,000 1921-22	310,201-314,000 1945-46	R plus five digits 1971-3
8,501-9,600 1904-05	83,001-101,775 1922-23	314,001-320,000 1946-47	
9,601-10,800 1905-06	101,776-124,600 1923-24	320,001-327,150 1947-48	**Saxophones Only**
10,801-12,000 1906-07	124,601-145,400 1924-25	327,151-332,150 1948-49	up to 83,000 . . .to end of 1976
12,001-13,000 1907-08	145,401-167,900 1925-26	332,151-337,250 1949-50	83,001-91,314 1976-77
13,001-15,400 1908-09	167,901-193,450 1926-27	337,251-341,850 1950-52	91,315-98,993 1977-78
15,401-17,800 1909-10	193,451-209,250 1927-28	341,851-354,742 1952-53	98,994-111,821 1978-79
17,801-21,200 1910-11	209,251-224,600 1928-29	354,743-359,251 1953-54	111,822-128,692 1979-80
	224,601-237,800 1929-30	359,252-500,001 1954-55	128,693-145,002 1980-81
	237,801-244,700 1930-31	500,002-571,750 1955-56	145,003-154,954 1981-82
	244,700-249,230 1931-32	571,751-652,002 1956-57	154,955-170,074 1982-83
	249,231-256,500 1932-33	652,003-718,626 1957-58	170,075-184,337 1983-84
	256,501-260,000 1933-34	718,627-779,657 1958-59	184,338-201,208 1984-85
	260,001-263,500 1934-35	779,658-834,200 1959-60	201,209-221,244 1985-86
	263,501-271,000 1935-36	834,201-898,556 1960-61	221,244-240,142 1986-87
	271,001-278,000 1936-37	898,557-999,999 1961-62	240,143-261,466 1987-88

Regiment Of New York brass band in 1873, and did much to popularise the still-novel saxophone in the US. Gilmore's band usually featured a three-man saxophone section playing baritone, alto and soprano. Following his collaboration with Conn in the late 1880s (it has been suggested, quite believably, that the Adolphe Sax instrument he brought with him to the US formed the basis of the first Conn saxophones), Lefébre also worked as a demonstration artist for Conn. After Gilmore died in 1892, Lefébre became the saxophone soloist in Sousa's band, a position Lefébre held until his own death in 1911.

In 1888, the same year that Conn introduced its first saxophone, the company's plant foreman Gus Buescher left to form the Buescher Band Instrument Co, and in 1907 Henry Martin's three sons left Conn to re-activate the Martin Band Instrument Co.

Around 1900 Conn ran a shortlived dedicated retail outlet in New York, and a patent for the new Conn Connqueror cornet was granted in 1901. Another fire, this one in 1910, destroyed another of Conn's factories, and a new plant was built nearby. At this time Conn dropped its Wonder line of instruments in favour of the New Wonder and New Invention models.

In 1915 Charles Conn sold his company to a group of investors headed by Carl Dimond Greenleaf, a successful flour-mill operator. Conn himself netted $1 million, an enormous sum at the time, and retired to California. (The new owners added the abbreviation "Ltd" to the company name, to make "C.G. Conn Ltd" – a useful dating clue to identify instruments made before or after 1915.) Greenleaf expanded Conn, adding to the company a repair school, a proper assembly line, a research laboratory, and an organ

production facility, and he laid the foundations for the US national school music programmes. By 1917 Conn had a workforce of 550 producing some 2,500 instruments per month.

Conn model names have included the Wonder, New Wonder, Connqueror and Connstellation lines, while musicians' own nicknames for Conn models have at various times included the "Big Bore" and the "Underslung" saxophones. Around 1919 Conn instigated a new model numbering system, with a letter indicating the instrument type – A for cornets, B for trumpets, H for slide trombones, M for saxophones – and an identifying numeral preceding this. Cornet model numbers include the 48-A (Superior Connqueror) and 80-A/85-A/92-A (Superior Victor). Saxophone model numbers include the 6-M (alto), 8-M (C-melody), 10-M (tenor), 12-M (baritone), 14-M (bass), 26-M (Connqueror alto)

Brass

Serial	Year	Serial	Year	Serial	Year
up to 700	to end of 1877	58,001-66,700	1900-01	219,851-230,900	1925-26
701-1,700	1877-78	66,701-71,000	1901-02	230,901-239,500	1926-27
1,701-3,000	1878-79	71,001-76,000	1902-03	239,501-252,900	1927-28
3,001-5,000	1879-80	76,001-82,000	1903-04	252,901-263,200	1928-29
5,001-6,000	1880-81	82,001-88,000	1904-05	263,201-273,700	1929-30
6,001-7,000	1881-82	88,001-94,000	1905-06	273,701-280,130	1930-31
7,001-8,000	1882-83	94,001-100,000	1906-07	280,131-281,360	1931-32
8,001-9,000	1883-84	100,001-106,000	1907-08	281,361-289,743	1932-33
9,001-10,500	1884-85	106,001-111,000	1908-09	289,744-294,687	1933-34
10,501-12,000	1885-86	111,001-116,000	1909-10	294,688-300,690	1934-35
12,001-13,000	1886-87	116,001-121,000	1910-11	300,691-307,996	1935-36
13,001-14,000	1887-88	121,001-126,000	1911-12	307,997-315,575	1936-37
14,001-16,500	1888-89	126,001-130,150	1912-13	315,576-322,650	1937-38
16,501-18,000	1889-90	130,151-132,400	1913-14	322,651-324,859	1938-39
18,001-20,000	1890-91	132,401-137,000	1914-15	324,860-327,850	1939-40
20,001-22,500	1891-92	137,001-142,575	1915-16	327,851-338,500	1940-41
22,501-25,000	1892-93	142,576-146,600	1916-17	338,501-348,150	1941-42
25,001-27,500	1893-94	146,601-155,000	1917-18	348,151-354,600	1942-43
27,501-29,000	1894-95	155,001-165,900	1918-19	354,601-355,500	1943-44
29,001-34,000	1895-96	165,901-169,500	1919-20	355,501-355,750	1944-45
34,001-40,000	1896-97	169,501-175,500	1920-21	355,751-355,850	1945-46
40,001-46,700	1897-98	175,501-190,450	1921-22	355,851-366,650	1946-47
46,701-52,000	1898-99	190,451-198,475	1922-23	366,651-376,100	1947-48
52,001-58,000	1899-1900	198,476-206,700	1923-24	376,101-383,650	1948-49
		206,701-219,850	1924-25	383,651-389,600	1949-50

Serial	Year
389,601-396,300	1950-51
396,301-408,000	1951-52
408,001-420,057	1952-53
420,058-427,301	1953-54
427,302-500,001	1954-55
500,002-571,850	1955-56
571,851-652,002	1956-57
652,003-718,626	1957-58
718,627-779,657	1958-59
779,658-834,200	1959-60
834,201-898,556	1960-61
898,557-949,465	1961-62
949,466-999,999	1962-63
A, B or C plus five digits	1963-4
D or E plus five digits	1964-5
F, G or H plus five digits	1965-6
J or K plus five digits	1966-7
L plus five digits	1967-8
M plus five digits*	1968-9
N plus five digits	1969-0
P plus five digits	1970-1
R plus five digits	1971-3

*Many much earlier saxophones have an M prefix simply to denote them as saxophones.

and 30-M (Connqueror tenor). Slide trombone model numbers include the 6-H (Artist Symphony), 20-H (Connquest) and 40-H/41-H/42-H (Ball-room). Trumpet model numbers include the 4-B (Symphony, New World Symphony), 13-B (Aida), 15-B (Director), 22-B (New Symphony) and 28-B (Connstellation).

Conn had introduced drawn-and-rolled tone-holes to saxophones in 1919, based on a December 1914 patent by flute manufacturer William Haynes, and this made for better instruments than those with conventional soldered-on toneholes. (Information concerning this patent is stamped on to many Conns made after this; the patent number 1119954 should not be confused with a serial number.) During the 1920s Conn dominated the booming saxophone business in the US along with its chief rival in this area, Buescher. By 1922 the company was turning out around 150 saxophones every day, and even introduced a shortlived option of coloured lacquer that created saxophones in bright colours.

A number of Conn saxophones from this period are noted for their fine engraving work, often featuring a woman's portrait (known as the "lady face" by players) and buildings in a landscape, as well as occasionally more ornate renderings. Talented engravers including Jake Gardner, Charles Stenberg and Julius Stenberg did this fine work at the Conn plant. While the company decided to stop using custom engraving at the end of the 1920s, Conn did continue to use several

standard machine-applied art deco patterns into the 1950s.

"Stencil" instruments were especially prevalent in the US saxophone boom of the 1920s, the term indicating the manufacture of instruments by one of the major makers – including Conn – stamped with a brandname to suit the customer. Thus Conn built saxophones and brass instruments bearing the names of Continental, Jenkins, Sears & Roebuck, Selmer (US), Wurlitzer, and York, among others. Conn also made their own cheaper brand of saxophones, Pan American. By the late 1920s the main Conn brand offered a line of saxophones that included Eb sopranino, C soprano, straight or curved Bb soprano, F mezzo-soprano, F Conn-O-Sax, Eb alto, C-melody, Bb tenor, baritone, and bass. However, by the calmer (and financially depressed) 1930s this was down to just the basic alto, tenor and baritone.

During World War II Conn effectively stopped instrument production and manufactured compasses, altimeters and other military-related items. This, coupled with a long strike in 1946 and 1947, resulted in Conn's weak post-war presence in the instrument market, although new lines did include the Connstellation brass models introduced around 1955. In 1949 Carl Greenleaf retired as Conn president, and the company, headed by Paul Gazlay in the 1950s, continued to founder. Piano and drum operations that had been purchased around 1930 were sold, and profitability generally suffered. Greenleaf's sons, Charles and

Leland, fought for supremacy; Leland won and became president in 1958; Charles left for Buescher. Conn suffered during the 1950s and 1960s, slipping in relation to competitors, becoming inefficient internally, and struggling financially – although they did manage to produce Conn's one-millionth brass instrument in 1963.

In 1969 in a hostile takeover bid C.G. Conn Ltd was acquired by Crowell-Collier Macmillan, better known as a publisher. Conn's existing president Leland Greenleaf left, and Macmillan installed Jack Latter as president. Latter considered the existing production facility unworkable and suggested moving out of Elkhart. So Conn's Elkhart factories were closed in 1970 (the buildings were sold to Selmer US the following year), and from 1970 until 1986 Conn's brass and wind instruments were manufactured in Abilene, Texas, with student instrument production moving to Japan. Problems continued, this time because the new Texas facility took time to get underway and the new workforce was unused to wind instrument manufacturing. Instruments from this period are renowned for poor workmanship.

In 1979 Macmillan appointed a new Conn president, Bill Cordier, in a final attempt to save the operation. Two years later, after Macmillan had suffered nearly six years of losses, Conn was sold to Daniel Henkin, a former Conn advertising manager. A few years later The Music Trades reported that this had been "the largest single sale of musical instrument manufacturing facilities to one individual". Despite moving the corporate offices back to Elkhart and introducing a Doc Severinsen trumpet, Henkin had no more luck with the business than had Macmillan, and in 1985 he sold Conn (as well as King and the Armstrong flute company) to Bernhard Muskantor. Muskantor formed United Musical Instruments (UMI) and quickly decided to close the Abilene factory, in 1986, moving flute and piccolo manufacturing to Elkhart and saxophone and brass manufacturing to the old King plant at Eastlake, near Cleveland, Ohio. Conn-brand instruments continue to appear today under the UMI umbrella, and include saxophones, trumpets, cornets, flugelhorns, trombones, French horns, tubas, sousaphones and other marching brass.

Conn serial number notes

Some Conn instruments have a letter above and below the serial number. On saxophones the top letter indicates the type of saxophone: A=alto, B=baritone, C=C-melody, Eb=sopranino, F=Conn-o-Sax or mezzo-soprano, S=soprano, T=tenor. On saxophones the lower letter indicates the pitch: L=(regular) low pitch; HP=high pitch.

Instruments manufactured 1887-97 are often marked "Elkhart and Worcester", a reference to Conn's Worcester, Massachusetts, factory in addition to the Elkhart, Indiana, factory.

Instruments manufactured 1897-1902 often bear references to both Conn's New York store and the Elkhart, Indiana, factory.

Instruments manufactured 1906-16 often bear a label with reference to the Metal Polishers, Buffers, Platers, Brass Moulders, Brass and Silver Workers union.

Instruments manufactured after 1915 are stamped "C.G. Conn Ltd" rather than simply "C.G. Conn".

Instruments sold during the 1930s and 1940s (at least) in Britain are often stamped with the importers name, Lafleur.

From 1974 to 1987 a new two-letter-prefix/five-digit serial number system was used for Conn brass, with a date code included within the first part of the number. The first letter indicates the decade: G for 1970s, H for 1980s. The second letter indicates the month of the year, from A for January through to L for December. The first digit indicates the year of the decade. The second digit indicates the type of instrument (1=cornet, 2=trumpet, 3=alto horn, 4=French horn, 5=mellophonium, 6=valve trombone, 7=slide trombone, 8=baritone horn/euphonium, 9=tuba, 0=sousaphone). The remaining three digits are the serial number for the individual instrument. For example, HA26485 indicates a valve trombone made in February 1982.

In 1988 the serial number reverted to an all-digit format, where the first two digits taken as a number, plus 50, reveal the last two digits of the production date. Thus a serial number beginning with 42... indicates (42+50=92) a production date of 1992.

Note that 1119954 appearing on many Conns is a patent number and not a serial number.

CONTINENTAL

See CONN.

COUESNON

This French firm of wind instrument manufacturers gained its name in the 1880s when Amédée Couesnon took over the running of his father-in-law's company, Gautrot, based in Château-Thierry, some 40 miles east of Paris. Under Couesnon's control the company expanded, operating from eight factories that built a large range of woodwind, string and brass instruments, and was among the first group of French manufacturers to build saxophones in the late 19th century in the wake of Adolphe Sax's achievements.

In the late 1920s the company built a few unusual saxophone-based instruments including the Saxie (which received a US patent in 1924) and the free-reed Couénophone (also known as the "Goofus"). Cuesnon also continued to produce good brass instruments.

After Cuesnon's death in 1951 the company declined, but was reorganised in the late 1960s and continues to produce trumpets, tubas, horns and French horns today, still based in Château-Thierry.

DEVILLE

See SELMER (PARIS).

ELKHART

See BUESCHER.

103

EVETTE & SCHAEFFER

See BUFFET CRAMPON.

CARL FISCHER

See BUESCHER.

GAUTROT

See COUESNON.

GETZEN

Anthony James (T.J.) Getzen started his own business in 1939 after training at Conn's band instrument repair school and working as a plant superintendent at Holton. Getzen's repair shop in Elkhorn, Wisconsin, started with three employees, and soon after World War II the company made the transition to manufacturing instruments, starting with trombones. Trumpets and cornets followed in 1947. Getzen's son, J. Robert, was appointed plant superintendent in 1949, and Getzen made bugles for the Drum & Bugle Corp. During the 1950s Getzen expanded to 80 employees, and concentrated on the student market.

J. Robert Getzen left in 1959 to start the Allied Music Corp repair shop, and then in the following year Getzen acquired the Hoosier Band Instrument Co of Elkhart, Indiana. Shortly afterwards Milwaukee businessman Harold M. Knowlton bought the Getzen Co from T.J. Getzen, founded a new factory, and introduced a complete line of Getzen professional cornets, flugelhorns and trumpets, and was helped in part by the trumpeter

Carl "Doc" Severinsen.

In the mid 1960s T.J. Getzen's son Donald left Getzen to form DEG Music Products in Lake Geneva, Wisconsin. J. Robert Getzen's Allied soon started to make bugles for DEG, and by 1972 were also supplying trumpets, cornets, trombones and marching brass. T.J. Getzen died in 1968.

In 1985 the Getzen company was bought from Knowlton by Charles F. Andrews, and Allied was bought from J. Robert Getzen by his sons, Tom and Ed (the latter also launching Edwards trombones at this time). In March 1991 Allied bought the assets of the failed Getzen Co, returning it to family ownership after 31 years. Getzen was made the parent manufacturing company, with Allied switching solely to a repair operation. The following year Getzen seriously entered the trombone market with a redesigned line, and this continues alongside the company's current lines of trumpets, flugelhorns, cornets and marching brass.

GLADIATOR

See KING.

GOUMAS

See BUFFET CRAMPON.

GRAFTON

Grafton was the brandname applied to a remarkable plastic saxophone produced in Britain during the 1950s. The man behind Grafton was Ettore Sommaruga.

Born in Milan, Italy in 1904, Sommaruga was an amateur mandolinist and guitarist and accomplished flute player who had been apprenticed to a brass musical instrument company in Milan.

Not caring for the rise of Fascism in Italy, Sommaruga moved to Paris in 1922 and got a job in a musical instrument factory where he became fascinated by the currently popular saxophone, and learnt how to plate metal. Four years later he moved to London to work at Hawkes & Co, the forerunner of Boosey & Hawkes, where his plating skills were valued, although by 1927 he was back in Paris, playing and fixing saxophones. It was at this time that Ettore anglicised his forename to Hector. By the early 1930s he was living in Spain, but in 1936 was back in England.

At the start of World War II Sommaruga was interned for three months as an enemy alien, on the Isle of Man, but after his release he made surgical instruments, working briefly in Grafton Way in central London – the source of his later saxophone brandname. With brass a scarce commodity at the end of the war, Sommaruga began experimenting with moulded plastic for musical instruments. A patent was applied for in 1945 and issued three years later for Sommaruga's plastic saxophone design, and finance was forthcoming from the musical instrument distribution company John E. Dallas.

Grafton Acrylic plastic alto saxophones began production at a factory in Bexleyheath, Kent, just south-east of London, and the first advertisements for the instruments appeared in Melody Maker in 1950, pitching the retail price at 55 guineas (£57.75, about $92), around half the price of a comparable conventional sax. In the US the Grafton Acrylic was distributed by the Gretsch company, starting in 1951.

It was certainly a striking instrument (see the pictures elsewhere in this book for the full effect). The neck and keys were metal, but the rest of the body was white plastic, with clear plastic key guards. It proves the theory that the brass used to manufacture conventional saxophones has little effect on the resulting sound of the instrument: Graftons sound distinctly saxophone-like.

Production is thought to have ceased quite quickly, around 1954, mainly due to a poor response to the unusual looks of the instrument, fears of damaging the

plastic, and a conservative reaction to the different feel of the Grafton's simplified key mechanism. During its short life the company also experimented with plastic tenor saxophones and clarinets.

Sommaruga had pulled out of the operation in 1953, and went to live in France again, later moving back to London, where he died in 1989. Five years later the Grafton Acrylic alto played briefly by Charlie Parker in the early 1950s fetched £114,000 (about $187,000) at an auction in London.

HOLTON

Frank Holton came to Chicago in 1893 as solo trombonist with John Philip Sousa's world-famous band to play at the Columbian Exposition. He decided to settle in the city and opened a small one-room Chicago shop in 1898, at first to make his trombone "slide"

oil that had the arresting name of Holton Electric Oil. But soon Holton began experiments in instrument design while he dabbled in used instrument sales and continued to play trombone.

Around 1900 the Holton company began making trombones (the first was called the Holton Special) and then cornets, trumpets, euphoniums and some percussion. By 1911 production had outgrown the company's existing factory of 30,000 square feet on Chicago's West Side. Holton already had a holiday home in Elkhorn, Wisconsin, and he decided to build a new factory there. Production began in spring 1918. Saxophones were soon added to the Holton line to satisfy the sax craze of the 1920s. Holton made a Rudy Wiedoeft model, named for the musician who did much to popularise the saxophone in America in the 1910s and pave the way for the 1920s boom.

105

HOLTON SERIAL NUMBERS 1900-1979				
Numbers listed in the left hand column of the chart below denote the approximate number range and the relevant production years are set in italic type on the right.	43,973-47,600 1919	101,400-105,199 1929	269,000-281,399 1955	
	47,601-49,817 1920	105,200-108,399 1930	281,400-293,699 1956	
	49,818-54,999 1921	108,400-111,049 1931	293,700-307,399 1957	
	55,000-55,249 1918	111,099-113,899 1932	307,400-315,699 1958	
	55,250-57,040 1919	113,990-114,999 1933	315,700-326,099 1959	
	57,041-58,499 1920	115,000-117,299 1934	326,100-337,599 1960	
	58,500-59,499 1921	117,300-118,599 1935	337,600-348,399 1961	
	59,500-60,599 1922	118,600-120,599 1936	348,400-358,499 1962	
001-254 1901	60,600-61,649 1923	120,600-122,899 1937	358,500-373,699 1963	
255-476 1902	61,650-62,199 1924	122,900-125,849 1938	373,700-388,949 1964	
477-526 1903	62,200-62,899 1925	125,850-132,799 1939	388,950-403,350 1965	
527-1,151 1904	62,900-63,149 1926	132,800-140,099 1940	403,351-435,999 1966	
1,152-1,872 1905	63,150-63,299 1927	140,100-151,299 1941	536,000-455,749 1967	
1,873-3,345 1906	63,300-63,549 1928	151,300-154,199 1942	455,750-467,099 1968	
3,346-4,630 1907	63,550-63,849 1929	154,200-154,699 1943	467,100-483,099 1969	
4,631-6,071 1908	63,850-64,049 1930	154,700-154,899 1944	483,100-496,799 1970	
6,072-9,474 1909	64,050-64,149 1931	154,900-156,099 1945	496,800-504,200 1971	
9,475-12,402 1910	70,000-70,549 1920	156,100-165,599 1946	504,201-519,299 1972	
12,403-15,950 1911	70,550-73,199 1921	165,600-181,999 1947	519,300-524,599 1973	
15,951-20,807 1912	73,200-76,099 1922	182,000-198,299 1948	524,600-529,899 1974	
20,808-21,100 1913	76,100-81,000 1923	198,300-210,299 1949	529,900-535,199 1975	
21,101-31,622 1914	81,001-85,600 1924	210,300-220,499 1950	535,200-541,999 1976	
31,623-33,671 1915	85,900-89,849 1925	220,500-232,599 1951	542,000-548,429 1977	
33,672-37,909 1916	89,850-92,799 1926	232,600-243,349 1952	548,430-553,524 1978	
37,910-41,069 1917	92,800-97,199 1927	243,350-254,099 1953	553,525-558,935 1979	
41,070-43,972 1918	97,200-101,399 1928	254,100-268,999 1954		

Meanwhile, Holton's "Guaranteed Plan" for schools ensured continuing sales there, and led to the company's Collegiate line of student instruments.

Demand for instruments fell during the hard times of the 1930s in the US, and with Holton himself ill the company's activities dwindled. When Frank Holton returned in 1939 production was at an all-time low, and he decided to sell his remaining stock to one Fred Kull. Holton died in 1942 at the age of 84.

By 1943 the company was involved in war work, and this provided happier times for Holton. This wartime boom left the company with a new owner, Elliot Kehl, with new engineering skills, and with increased efficiency. A retraining programme for staff now unused to musical instrument making led to an increase in quality of Holton wind instruments, and Holton's Arvid Walters designed many of the new lines that appeared at the time. By the mid 1950s Holton boasted four lines: the top-line Stratodyne and Revelation instruments, and the Super-Collegiate and Collegiate student instruments.

In 1964 Kehl was approached by Vito Pascucci of the Leblanc corporation, himself an ex-apprentice of Holton, and Holton was purchased by Leblanc that year. Today, the Holton line includes trumpets, cornets and flugelhorns, and the company is the largest producer of French horns in the world. Holton's chief instrument designer is Larry Ramirez.

Multi-instrumentalist Maynard

Ferguson began an association with Holton in the 1970s – the company briefly built then his unusual "superbone", a combination of slide and valve trombone – and at present Holton also offer a line of five Ferguson-endorsed trumpet models.

JENKINS

See CONN.

KEILWERTH

See BOOSEY & HAWKES.

KING

King originated as a brandname used by the H.N. White company of Cleveland, Ohio. Henderson N. White grew up in Detroit, Michigan, and worked as a boy in the Berdan musical instrument repair shop there. He soon moved to Cleveland to head up the repair shop at McMillin's music store, and after five years branched out on his own to set up in business with a partner, C.H. Berg.

In 1893 White became sole owner of the operation, and the following year, in collaboration

with a local trombonist, Thomas King, built the first King-brand trombone, a tenor model with an improved slide mechanism. White's brother Hugh joined the company in 1903, and soon his son Richard also began working for the business. By 1924 the H.N. White company employed 200 workers in 38,000 square feet of factories at Superior Avenue in Cleveland (a location first used in 1909), producing King trombones, trumpets, cornets and other brass instruments, as well as saxophones which were enjoying tremendous popularity at the time.

White had imported Evette & Schaeffer saxophones from France at the end of the 1900s, and began to produce their own King saxophones in the mid 1910s, starting with an alto model in 1916. By 1923 the King line also included C-melody, tenor, baritone and soprano instruments, and three years later they added the curved-soprano-like Saxello. From the mid 1920s and into the early 1930s White divided their saxophone line into three brands: King continued, and was top of the line; Cleveland was added as a mid-price brand; and American

KING SERIAL NUMBERS 1893-1975

Numbers listed in the left hand column of the chart below denote the approximate number range and the relevant production years are set in italic type on the right.

001-50,000	*1893-1915*
50,001-78,000	*1915-25*
78,001-126,000	*1925-30*
126,001-176,000	*1930-35*
176,001-186,000	*1935-36*
186,001-200,000	*1936-37*
200,001-212,000	*1937-38*
212,001-225,000	*1938-39*
225,001-239,000	*1939-40*
239,001-254,000	*1940-41*
254,001-264,000	*1941-42*
264,001-267,500	*1942-45*
267,501-277,000	*1945-46*
277,001-287,000	*1946-47*
287,001-296,500	*1947-48*
296,501-301,500	*1948-49*
301,501-308,000	*1949-50*
308,001-316,500	*1950-51*
316,501-322,000	*1951-52*
322,001-330,000	*1952-53*
330,001-337,000	*1953-54*
337,001-340,000	*1954-55*
340,001-370,000	*1955-60*
370,001-406,500	*1960-65*
406,501-457,600	*1965-70*
457,601-511,751	*1970-75*

106

Standard and Gladiator became White's cheap student lines.

New King saxophone models appeared in the early 1930s after this reorganisation, the first being the Voll-True (1930), and then the Voll-True II (1933) which had a new bore design and repositioned toneholes. In the mid 1930s these models were renamed Zephyr, and then superseded by a new design, the Zephyr Special (1938) which had a more comfortable key design (the keys looked good, too, with pearl inlays) and a solid silver neck – the first King sax model with this distinctive feature.

After World War II King came out with a new saxophone model, the revered Super-20, effectively an enhanced Zephyr Special. Changes included an underslung octave mechanism. The Super-20 quickly became established as a favourite of the late 1940s and into the 1960s, its distinctive silver neck and bell and pearl-inlaid keys making it an elegant accompaniment to many a jazz stylist. The King Silver Flair trumpet also found favour with a number of jazz players at this time.

White was sold in 1965 to Nathan Dolan Associates and quickly became a subsidiary of the Seeburg company. The operation faltered in comparison to its former glories, and in 1966 production of White's instruments was moved to Eastlake, Ohio. The Super-20 saxophones continued in production until 1975, and White's student lines continued, but by the early 1980s sax manufacturing was halted, and only brass instruments were made. In 1983 King was bought by Bernhard

Muskantor, who soon acquired Armstrong flutes and Conn, and formed United Musical Instruments (UMI), under whose umbrella King-brand saxophones, trumpets, cornets, trombones and other brass instruments continue in production today.

LYON & HEALY

See BUESCHER and MARTIN.

MARTIN

The Martin Band Instrument Company was established by Henry Martin in Chicago around 1890, but production was interrupted by the great Chicago Fire of 1906. In that year the company was re-established by Martin's sons in Elkhart, Indiana, after they had left their employment at the Conn company.

"Stencil" instruments were especially prevalent in the US saxophone boom in the 1920s; the term indicates the manufacture by one of the major makers – including Martin – of instruments with a brandname to suit the customer. Thus Martin built saxophones and brass instruments for Lyon & Healy, Selmer US (Manhattan models) and Wurlitzer, among others.

The Martin Committee trumpet became a favourite among jazz musicians from the 1950s. Martin saxophone models include the fine Committee and Magna, the Indiana, the Handcraft and the Medalist, as well as the unusual and shortlived button-keyed "Typewriter" model. The Committee saxophone was

developed by a committee of musicians that included Norman C. Bates, Lyall Bowen, Steve Broadus, Joseph Gillespie, Vic Hauprich, Saxie Mansfield, Ollie Thomas, and Joseph Usifer. Post-World War II Martin saxophones are often of first-rate quality.

The Martin company was sold in 1965 to the Wurlitzer company, and six years later was purchased by Leblanc and moved to Kenosha, Wisconsin, where Martin-brand Committee trumpets and Urbie Green trombones as well as cornets and flugelhorns continue in production today.

MONETTE

David Monette began his career as a band instrument repairman in Salem, Oregon, in 1978. Applying his knowledge as both a trumpet player and an instrument technician he built the first Monette trumpet in May 1983 in Bloomington, Indiana, at the age of 27. Monette's first few instruments were bought and endorsed by top classical players, including Adolph Herseth (principal trumpet, Chicago Symphony) and Charles Schlueter (principal trumpet, Boston Symphony).

After moving to downtown Chicago in 1984 Monette started working with jazz players too, and musicians such as Wynton Marsalis, Art Farmer and Guy Barker sought him out to design and build new instruments.

As his trumpets evolved, Monette started to work on an improved mouthpiece design that would deal with the problems of inconsistent pitch centre apparent with existing units. Monette's first constant-pitch-centre trumpet mouthpieces were made in 1986. This innovation led Monette to what he describes as "radically improved" instrument designs, including the Raja and Raja Samadhi, the only modern brass instruments designed with integral mouthpieces.

In 1990 Monette invented a new instrument, a hybrid trumpet/flugelhorn called the flumpet, which has been used by a number of jazz, solo and symphonic performers. Currently located in Portland, Oregon, David Monette produces his instruments with seven co-workers.

OLDS

Olds is a brandname most associated with some fine

trombones built from the early 20th century onwards. Frank Ernest Olds, a trombonist himself, started the F.E. Olds business in 1908 in California. His son Reginald joined the operation in 1931, when "& Son" was added to the company name. Still in California, the company began to add other brass instruments to the line, including trumpets. Olds brass model names include Recording, Special, Super, Opera, and student Ambassador line (which included saxophones).

Olds merged with the Reynolds brass instrument company in 1964; both were purchased by Norlin in 1970. The present owners of the Olds name bought the business in 1980, and F.E. Olds & Son Inc are today based in New Jersey, although their manufacturing operation is in Elkhart, Indiana.

PAN AMERICAN

See CONN.

REYNOLDS

See OLDS.

SAX

Antoine-Joseph Sax, known to all as Adolphe Sax, was a prolific inventor. The saxophone was just one of many musical instruments he devised, but where the others usually had rivals or were developments of earlier ideas – and often came to nothing – the saxophone was a new invention that fully deserves the incorporation of Sax's surname, and of course is still in wide use today.

Adolphe Sax was born in

108

OLDS/REYNOLDS SERIAL NUMBERS TO 1979

Numbers listed in the left hand column of the chart below denote the approximate number range and the relevant production years are set in italic type on the right.

F. E. Olds

up to 73,000	to end of March 1952
73,001-80,000	March-July 1952
80,001-90,000	July 1952-February 1953
90,001-100,000	February-October 1953
100,001-150,000	October 1953-August 1955
150,001-200,000	August 1955-November 1956
200,001-250,000	November 1956-July 1958
250,001-300,000	July 1958-September 1959
300,001-350,000	September 1959-June 1960
350,001-400,000	June 1960-March 1962
400,001-450,000	March 1962-February 1964
450,001-500,000	February 1964-February 1965
500,001-550,000	February 1965-June 1966
550,001-600,000	June 1966-June 1967
600,001-650,000	June 1967-June 1968
650,001-700,000	June 1968-June 1969
700,001-750,000	June 1969-June 1971
750,001-800,000	June 1971-June 1972
800,001-850,000	June 1972-October 1973
850,001-900,000	October 1973-November 1974
900,001-950,000	November 1974-April 1976
950,001-970,000	April 1976-September 1976
970,001-990,000	September 1976-March 1977
990,001-999,999	March-September 1977

Reynolds

up to 200,000	to end of November 1964
200,001-210,000	November 1964-November 1965
210,001-220,000	November 1965-October 1966
220,001-230,000	October 1966-July 1967
230,001-240,000	July 1967-May 1968
240,001-250,000	May 1968-November 1969
250,001-260,000	November 1969-April 1971
260,001-270,000	April 1971-August 1972
270,001-280,000	August 1972-October 1973
280,001-290,000	October 1973-June 1974
290,001-300,000	June 1974-September 1975
300,001-310,000	September 1975-August 1976
310,001-314,587	August-October 1977

F.E. Olds / Reynolds

A00001-A05266	October 1977-December 1977
A05267-A06741	December 1977-January 1978
A06742-A10066	January-February 1978
A10067-A12537	February-March 1978
A12538-A16496	March-April 1978
A16497-A18163	April-May 1978
A18164-A20876	May-June 1978
A20877-A24530	June-July 1978
A24531-A24606	July-August 1978
A24607-A28375	August-September 1978
A28376-A31565	September-October 1978
A31566-A34616	October-November 1978
A34617-A37470	November-December 1978
A37471-A40550	December 1978-January 1979

Belgium in 1814, the son of a brass and woodwind instrument maker, Charles-Joseph Sax, who had a distinct influence on many of his son's later achievements. Adolphe became a music student at the Royal School of Singing, studying vocals, flute and clarinet, and soon became adept at the latter two. Although he did continue to play, Sax decided to join the family instrument firm, and at the age of just 16 some of his handiwork was displayed at the 1830 Brussels Industrial Exhibition. He worked on modifications of the clarinet, developing a successful bass version. Around this time Adolphe also began experimenting with valved bugle-horns (these would become known as "saxhorns"), as well as an instrument that took a single-reed mouthpiece similar to that of the clarinet and combined it with a conical metal tube. This would become the saxophone.

Adolphe moved to Paris in 1842, assisted and encouraged by the French military, who saw the potential of his instruments for military bands, and by composers and musicians such as Hector Berlioz. Working at the same time as other French makers building custom valved brass instruments, Sax brought with him to Paris ideas for his new "families" of instruments. His matched valved bugles, or "saxhorns", first demonstrated in 1844 and patented in 1845, did much to assist the wind band (and in particular the British brass band through the musical and commercial efforts of the Distin

family). Adolphe's saxophone was first demonstrated as a bass instrument, around 1842, and was patented in 1846. It is possible that Sax hit on the idea for the saxophone by combining the single-reed mouthpiece of his bass clarinet with an ophicleide, a bass brass instrument of the keyed-bugle family that had been around since the 1820s.

Having set up a factory to produce his instruments in Paris, Sax found himself hounded by jealous rivals displeased by his operations. Sax was overrun with business difficulties and legal assaults for the rest of his life. Press campaigns were adopted and key workers lured away from the Sax factory. In one incident Sax's servant was murdered in what may have been a case of mistaken identity. The opposition to Sax escalated in 1845 when, after a public contest, the French military decided to make the use of saxhorns and saxophones compulsory in French military bands, effectively creating a monopoly for Sax. French instrument manufacturers (including Besson – see earlier entry) were enraged by the success of this upstart foreigner.

By the 1850s saxophones were being made by Sax in a range of six sizes, equivalent to the modern sopranino to bass. Sax became Professor of Saxophone at the Paris Conservatoire in 1857, where he continued to teach for 13 years. Sax's patents expired in the 1860s, and copies of his instruments began to appear. By the following decade Sax's fortunes had gone

into terminal decline, and in 1877 he was declared bankrupt for the last time. The factory was closed and goods and machinery were sold. Adolphe Sax died in 1894 at the age of 80. His sons Charles and Adolphe Jr. continued a manufacturing business on a much reduced basis, but the Sax factories were sold to Selmer in the early 1920s. Selmer did produce a line of "Adolphe" saxophones, still advertised as late as the early 1930s in Britain, but started to make their own Selmer-brand saxophones a few years later.

SCHILKE

Renold Schilke began to learn to play the cornet in the 1910s, and worked for the Holton instrument company in the early 1920s. He became a professional cornet player, and began working with the Chicago Symphony Orchestra in 1929, continuing into the 1960s. Schilke started experimental trumpet manufacturing from the 1920s, and worked with the Benge company from 1934 to 1952.

In 1956 Schilke began his own brass instrument manufacturing business, aiming at the high-end professional player. In 1966 Schilke became a consultant to the Yamaha company of Japan, and in 1975 Schilke's own company began horn production. Renold Schilke died in 1982. The present Schilke company is based in Illinois and continues to produce instruments.

109

SCHILKE SERIAL NUMBERS TO 1976

Up to 1961 Schilke instruments were marked with the date of completion as the serial number: the month first, the date of the month second, and the last two digits of the year last. For example, a trumpet with serial number 4859 was completed on April 8th 1959. From 1961 the following numbers applied.

Numbers listed in the left hand column of the chart below denote the approximate number range and the relevant production years are set in italic type on the right.

Range	Year	Range	Year	Range	Year
1,110-1,212	*1961*	1,509-1,570	*1967*	7,347-7,361	*1976*
1,213-1,218	*1962*	1,571-1,575	*1964*	7,362-7,594	*1975*
1,219-1,221	*1961*	1,600-1,629	*1969*	7,595-7,613	*1976*
1,222-1,225	*1962*	1,630-1,999	*1970*	7,614-7,713	*1975*
1,226-1,269	*1961*	2,000-2,044	*1963*	7,714-7,723	*1976*
1,270-1,281	*1963*	2,045-2,220	*1964*	7,724-7,736	*1975*
1,282-1,285	*1962*	2,221-2,226	*1965*	7,737-7,747	*1976*
1,286-1,290	*1961*	2,227-2,234	*1966*	7,762-7,769	*1976*
1,291-1,302	*1963*	2,235-2,236	*1967*	7,770-7,793	*1975*
1,303-1,422	*1962*	2,237-2,510	*1965*	7,794-8,595	*1976*
1,423-1,508	*1963*	2,511-2,766	*1966*	20,401-20,496	*1970*
		2,767-2,846	*1967*	20,497-20,899	*1971*
		2,847-2,858	*1968*	20,900-20,971	*1972*
		2,859-3,143	*1967*	21,001-21,016	*1972*
		3,144-3,609	*1968*	21,017-21,047	*1971*
		3,610-3,618	*1969*	21,048-21,052	*1972*
		3,619-3,647	*1968*	21,053-21,074	*1973*
		3,648-4,163	*1969*	21,075-21,090	*1974*
		4,164-4,637	*1970*	21,091-21,099	*1973*
		4,638-4,649	*1971*	21,100-21,421	*1972*
		4,650-4,703	*1970*	22,318-23,139	*1974*
		4,704-5,255	*1971*	23,140-23,359	*1975*
		5,256-5,816	*1972*	23,360-23,367	*1976*
		5,817-6,293	*1973*	23,400-23,985	*1975*
		6,294-6,923	*1974*	23,986-24,635	*1976*
		6,924-7,346	*1975*	24200A-24300A	*1976*

SEARS & ROEBUCK

See CONN.

SELMER (PARIS)

Johannes Jacobus Zelmer was a drum major in the French military toward the end of the 18th century, and his son Jean-Jacques Selmer, despite respelling his name, followed Johannes's trade and became the army's Chef de la Musique (Head of Music). Jean-Jacques's son Charles-Frederic had 16 children, and the family's musical heritage was most evident in Charles-Emile, Alexandre-Gabriel and Henri-Chery, the latter two set to become fine clarinet players. Henri Selmer, born in 1858, began his musical career by studying clarinet at the Paris Conservatoire in 1880. He became a member (briefly) of the Garde Republicaine band, and also of the Orchestre de l'Opéra Comique.

Henri Selmer soon developed a talent for cutting clarinet reeds, both for his own purposes and for his fellow clarinetists, and his custom reeds quickly became popular. He set up a small workshop to make them, and then started to produce mouthpieces, gaining a good reputation for these, too. With the establishment of Henri Selmer & Cie in 1885 the story of Selmer musical instruments was underway.

By 1890 Henri was continuing with his workshop, making reeds and mouthpieces, and had also begun adjusting, repairing and modifying clarinets – which led him to consider manufacturing. So he set up a factory to make clarinets, soon employing around 20 workers at a building in Place Dancourt in Paris.

Henri's brother Alexandre Selmer (born 1864) had gone to the United States in 1895 and worked as a clarinet soloist with

the Boston Symphony, the Cincinnati Symphony, and, most prestigiously, the New York Philharmonic Orchestra. Around 1900 Alexandre opened an instrument store on Third Avenue in New York – the origin of the Selmer US company – and secured an agent in Britain, Gomez. Selmer US was established under the official name of H&A Selmer in 1904. Thus Selmer Paris instruments soon became successful across the Atlantic. Shown at an exhibition in Saint Louis, Missouri, they were awarded a gold medal. The international potential for Selmer Paris instruments was becoming clear.

Back in France, Henri Selmer decided that the time was right to extend the company's activities beyond clarinet making. Competing instrument makers in France at the time included two big names: Evette & Schaeffer, who also used the Buffet-Crampon brand; and Couesnon, who built in large quantities and exported to the US. During the 1910s Henri extended the Selmer line into a family of clarinets, as well as bassoons and oboes. From 1910 to 1918 the Selmer workshops were situated at Méru, just north of Paris, and the company also used a steam shop at Gaillon, nearer Rouen.

In 1918 Alexandre decided to return to France from the US, and left George Bundy, one of his clarinet pupils, in his place in New York, having sold to Bundy the distribution rights for Selmer Paris instruments imported into the US, as well as the business in US-made instruments, including the Selmer American Model series. Bundy added a line of Selmer US flutes, and in 1927 established Selmer US's own manufacturing base in Elkhart, Indiana. Elkhart was already established as the wind instrument capital of the US, as home to the production of Conn and Buescher instruments among others. (The operation of the Selmer US and the later Selmer UK companies sometimes confuses players who find one of the instruments marketed by these firms, and think that they must have a fine Selmer Paris instrument. Selmer Paris instruments are the only ones from the mid 1920s onward that bear clear markings indicating their French origins!)

Among the workers at the Selmer factory were Paul Lefèvre and his sons Maurice and Henri. When in 1914 Henri left for the war with a homemade saxophone in his kit bag, Henri Selmer is said to have noted the saxophone as a potential addition to the Selmer line of instruments.

By 1919 Henri had decided to build a new factory at Mantes, just west of Paris, where Evette & Schaeffer were already established. The Lefèvres were responsible for production at the new site. Henri Selmer's son Maurice joined the company at this time, and Maurice Selmer and Henri Lèfevre developed machinery at the new factory. Around this time Henri furthered his intention to make saxophones by purchasing the Adolphe Sax factories from Sax's sons Charles and Adolphe. Selmer sold saxophones made at the Sax plant, as well as instruments made for them by the Evette & Schaeffer firm. But at the end of 1921 (on the 31st December, according to company legend) the Selmer Model 22 alto appeared, the first completely Selmer-made saxophone – although it bore clear Sax influences. Trumpets were also added to the Selmer line later in the 1920s – the Special Challenger trumpet would later gain support from a number of jazz musicians – and the less Sax-like Selmer Model 26 saxophone followed around 1926.

In 1929 Selmer appointed Ben Davis as the UK agent for Selmer, after the British saxophonist had played in Paris and met up with Selmer managers. Davis's British-based Selmer operation would continue to the late 1960s, acquiring wider distribution rights (and also at various times acting as UK agent for Vincent Bach, Martin, Olds and King instruments).

Around 1930 Selmer first sold their new large-bore Super Sax model, sometimes also called the Super Model but generally known today as the "Cigar Cutter" thanks to a small, purely decorative, circular cut-out on the octave key post. But it was the totally new design of Selmer's Balanced Action saxophone, introduced in the mid 1930s, that really began to underline Selmer's serious assault on the saxophone market. The Balanced Action had a redesigned key system (especially the bottom action keys and connectors) and repositioned bell keys on the right-hand side. It offered a commanding, powerful sound – what Selmer described as "bite". The design of the Balanced Action would lead clearly to the company's revered Mark VI models which first appeared in the 1950s.

Henri Selmer died in July 1941, and Maurice Selmer took over the running of Selmer Paris. During World War II there was a limited supply of materials and, of course, a limited potential for exporting. The company's musical activities were significantly reduced, and at one point manufactured bicycle pumps. In America the Selmer US operation had Buescher build them an odd "Padless" saxophone in the early 1940s. But in the aftermath of the war Maurice began to rebuild Selmer Paris and started to offer a full line of models again.

The first new post-war model offered by Selmer Paris, building on the good work of the pre-war Balanced Action model, was the Super Action saxophone. This refined some of the Balanced Action features and had a reproportioned neck, but most

SELMER PARIS SERIAL NUMBERS 1922-1987

Numbers listed in the left hand column of the chart below denote the approximate number range and the relevant production years are set in italic type on the right.

Trumpets

up to 251	to end of *1931*
252-265	*1931-32*
266-571	*1932-33*
572-785	*1933-34*
786-1,177	*1934-35*
1,178-1,459	*1935-36*
1,460-1,633	*1936-37*
1,634-1,979	*1937-38*
1,980-2,472	*1938-39*
2,473-3,146	*1939-40*
3,147-3,350	*1940-41*
3,351-3,380	*1941-42*
3,381-3,939	*1942-43*
3,940-4,160	*1943-44*
4,161-4,308	*1944-45*
4,309-4,700	*1945-46*
4,701-5,409	*1946-47*
5,410-6,441	*1947-48*
6,442-7,477	*1948-49*
7,478-8,521	*1949-50*
8,522-9,641	*1950-51*
9,642-10,569	*1951-52*
10,570-12,200	*1952-53*
12,201-13,600	*1953-54*
13,601-15,000	*1954-55*
15,001-16,900	*1955-56*
16,901-18,402	*1956-57*
18,403-19,839	*1957-58*
19,840-21,223	*1958-59*
21,224-23,038	*1959-60*

Saxophones

750-1,400	*1922*
1,401-2,350	*1923*
2,351-3,350	*1924*
3,351-4,450	*1925*
4,451-5,600	*1926*
5,601-7,850	*1927*
7,851-9,700	*1928*
9,701-11,950	*1929*
11,951-14,000	*1930*
14,001-15,750	*1931*
15,751-17,250	*1932*
17,251-18,700	*1933*
18,701-20,100	*1934*
20,101-21,750	*1935*
21,751-22,650	*1936*
22,651-25,600	*1937*
25,601-27,650	*1938*
27,651-29,300	*1939*
29,301-29,750	*1940*
29,751-30,500	*1941*
30,501-31,150	*1942*
31,151-31,580	*1943*
31,581-31,850	*1944*
31,851-32,350	*1945*
32,351-33,700	*1946*
33,701-35,800	*1947*
35,801-38,500	*1948*
38,501-41,500	*1949*
41,501-45,100	*1950*
45,101-48,300	*1951*
48,301-51,800	*1952*
51,801-55,200	*1953*
55,201-59,000	*1954*
59,001-63,400	*1955*
63,401-68,900	*1956*
68,901-74,500	*1957*
74,501-80,400	*1958*
80,401-85,200	*1959*
85,201-91,300	*1960*
91,301-97,300	*1961*
97,301-104,500	*1962*
104,501-112,500	*1963*
112,501-121,600	*1964*
121,601-131,800	*1965*
131,801-141,500	*1966*
141,501-152,400	*1967*
152,401-162,500	*1968*
162,501-173,800	*1969*
173,801-184,900	*1970*
184,901-196,000	*1971*
196,001-208,700	*1972*
208,701-220,800	*1973*
220,801-233,900	*1974*
233,901-246,800	*1975*
246,801-261,100	*1976*
261,101-276,100	*1977*
276,101-289,700	*1978*
289,701-303,100	*1979*
303,101-315,500	*1980*
315,001-327,300	*1981*
327,301-340,200	*1982*
340,201-353,300	*1983*
353,301-366,400	*1984*
366,401-378,800	*1985*
378,801-391,000	*1986*
391,801-406,000	*1987*

Selmer Serial Number Notes

Recent data are not available, but by the mid 1990s saxophone serial numbers were up to at least 530,000. A Selmer ad of 1962 suggested that the first Mark VI instrument had number 53,727. This would place the instrument in 1953; however, today Selmer's official date of introduction for the Mark VI is given as1954.

112

notably featured a radical new design that for the first time featured offset keys. Until the Super Action, all saxophone toneholes and the associated keys were in-line; now the keys were offset, positioned to sit more comfortably under the player's hands. The Super Action was also the first saxophone with a detachable bell, which made repairs and maintenance easier.

Alexandre Selmer died in 1951. Selmer Paris's saxophone masterstroke, the Mark VI, appeared in 1954. It achieved an ergonomic facility which many players still believe to be unsurpassed in modern saxophone design. Help in devising the Mark VI came from the French virtuoso classical saxophonist Marcel Mule. During World War I he played in a military band and later the Garde Republicaine, building a worldwide reputation as its saxophone soloist and organising their saxophone quartet, which after 1936 was known as the Paris Saxophone Quartet. This group did much to publicise the saxophone's classical capabilities. In 1942 the Paris Conservatoire invited Mule to become the director of a new saxophone class, which had been defunct since Adolphe Sax last taught there in 1870. Mule held the post until 1968, and his study materials are still in use today.

The Mark VI, which came out of Mule's collaboration with Selmer Paris, built on the achievements of the Balanced Action and Super Action designs, adding a new octave mechanism and improvements to the bottom action. It was the peak of Selmer's post-war saxophone design, and combined all the best features in a supremely ergonomic instrument that has attracted and still attracts many of the finest saxophone players throughout the world. A fine example of a Mark VI is a prized and often expensive find today.

The Mark VI remained as Selmer's saxophone model until 1974, when a new Mark VII was introduced, first shown by the company at the Congrès de Saxophone at Bordeaux. Apparently jazzman Johnny Griffin – up to then a King Super-20 player –helped Selmer with the initial design, but reports suggest that he was unhappy with the final result. There were good ideas evident in the changes made to the Mark VII, including a new type of "pinned" connection rod for the keys, and a better tuning stability. But the keywork had been respaced, and for many players the Mark VII lacked the positive feel of its predecessor.

Selmer improved the key spacing and changed the neck and bore for their new Super Action 80 model (alto and tenor models were introduced in 1981, with baritone and soprano following a few years later), while the more recent Super Action 80 Series II (1986) and Series III (1997) models have in some players' opinions got Selmer Paris closer to the Mark VI feel.

Maurice Selmer had died in 1961. Henri Lefèvre became president, but was tragically killed in an accident in 1968, and Georges Selmer took his place, assisted by his brothers Jean and Jacques. Jean's son Patrick Selmer joined the company in 1973 and became responsible for marketing and PR. Selmer Paris and Selmer US continue in business today.

Selmer used a variety of brandnames for its cheaper, student lines through the years, including Signet and Deville. George Bundy, who had taken over the Selmer US business in the US when Alexandre Selmer returned to Paris in 1918, instigated a subsidiary brand of instruments marketed by Selmer US from around 1930, using his own surname as a brandname. At first the Bundy line consisted of items imported into the US from various sources, some of good quality, but later Selmer made their own Bundy instruments in the US. After Selmer bought Bach in 1961 and Buescher in 1963 it attempted to absorb some elements from these two companies' instruments into the line of student Bundy-brand instruments, leaning on Bach for the trumpets and brass and on Buescher for the saxophones. Selmer's US-made Bundy instruments are not well regarded. The Bundy* brand was dropped by Selmer US during the 1990s.

Note for Bundy serial numbers see Buescher.

SELMER UK

See SELMER (PARIS).

SELMER US

See BUESCHER, CONN, MARTIN and SELMER (PARIS).

SIGNET

See SELMER (PARIS).

H.N. WHITE

See KING.

WILLIAMS

See CALICCHIO.

WURLITZER

See BUESCHER, CONN and MARTIN.

YAMAHA

In 1887 Torakusu Yamaha began producing reed organs in Hamamatsu, central Japan. Ten years later he founded a company called Nippon Gakki (Musical Instruments of Japan). Around the same time, a Tokyo boilermaker began making bugles and established a wind instrument company named Nippon Kangakki (Japanese Wind Instruments) using the Nikkan brand. Both companies were active in popularising western musical instruments in Japan, and in 1965 jointly developed the first wind instrument to bear the Yamaha name.

By 1970 the two firms had merged, and in 1972 Yamaha started to develop wind instruments jointly with the Vienna Philharmonic Orchestra. By 1975 Yamaha was claiming that it had the biggest wind instrument factory in the world. Yamaha's fine YS line of saxophones was launched in 1980, and includes the good YS-62 model.

113

In 1987, while commemorating its 100th anniversary year, Yamaha's official company name was changed to the Yamaha Corporation, and during 1991 Yamaha produced its five-millionth wind instrument. A year earlier Yamaha had introduced its new Custom series of saxophones.

YANAGISAWA

Yanagisawa was established in Japan in 1893 as a pioneering wind repair shop, and soon began to manufacture brass instruments such as bugles and traditional Japanese instruments. After World War II the repair shop benefited from the many American servicemen's instruments that crossed its benches, and the company's first saxophone model was produced in 1954, the T-3 tenor. It is has been suggested that this first silver-plated model was bought by an American serviceman in Tokyo. Yanagisawa's first alto, the A-3, followed in 1956. Design influence was clearly centred on

114

YANAGISAWA SERIAL NUMBERS 1970s-1993

During the 1970s a date code was put into the serial number. The third and fourth digits reveal the last two digits of the date: for example, 1272903 = 1972, 12781317 = 1978, and so on. Serials from 1980 to 1993 are shown below.

Numbers listed in the left hand column of the chart right denote the approximate number range and the relevant production years are set in italic type on the right.

Serial	Year
up to 00102143	*to end of 1980*
00102144-00106981	*1981*
00106982-00111892	*1982*
00111893-00117142	*1983*
00117143-00122663	*1984*
00122664-00128485	*1985*
00128486-00134903	*1986*
00134904-00141658	*1987*
00141659-00148774	*1988*
00148775-00156006	*1989*
00156007-00162968	*1990*
00162969-00170073	*1991*
00170074-00177117	*1992*
00177118-00184318	*1993*

the ubiquitous Selmer Mark VI.

A redesigned alto, the A-5, appeared in 1965, and the T-4 and T-5 tenors and A-4 alto were introduced in the following year. Gradually Yanagisawa began to develop its own character, and the company's first baritone (and indeed the first to be made in Japan), the B-6, joined the line in 1967. Two years later a soprano, the S-6, completed the regular saxophone family.

The next step was to build a sopranino instrument, and this was added to the Yanagisawa line in 1972 – the first one is owned by Sonny Rollins – and a curved

soprano came along in 1979. Around this time two new series of alto and tenor saxes, the 500 and 800, were introduced, and these continued until the introduction of the 900 series in 1992 and the more recent 990 series. The soprano was first offered in 1985 with an interchangeable straight or curved neck.

YORK

See CONN.

ENDS

117

OWNERS' CREDITS

Instruments photographed came from the following individuals' and organisations' collections and stocks, and we are most grateful for their help.

The owners are listed here in the alphabetical order of the code used to identify their instruments in the Key To Instrument Photographs below.

AG Alex Garnett; **BI** Bill Lewington Ltd; **DF** Digby Fairweather; **GA** Garnett Woodwind; **GB** Guy Barker; **JM** Jacquie Martin; **PH** Phil Parker Ltd; **TB** Tony Bingham; **WG** Willie Garnett.

KEY TO INSTRUMENT PHOTOGRAPHS

The following key is designed to identify who owned which instruments when they were photographed for this book. After the relevant page number (in italic type) we list: the instrument, followed by the owner's initials in **bold type** (see Owners' Credits above). For example, "11: Butler cornet **DF**" means that the Butler cornet on page 11 was owned by Digby Fairweather.

11: Butler cornet **DF**. 11/12: King cornet **DF**; Conn cornet **DF**. 16: Selmer trumpet **DF**. 20/21: Bach trumpet **PH**. 21: King trombone **BI**. 24/25: Martin trumpet **PH**. 25: Besson flugelhorn **PH**. 28: Blessing mellophonium **DF**. 28/29: Monette trumpet **GB**. 29: Monette flumpet **GB**. 31: Sax baritone **TB**. 32: Sax tenor **TB**. 33/34: Sax alto **TB**. 34: Sax soprano **TB**. 35: Conn C-melody **GA**. 42: Buescher tenor **AG**. 43: Buescher alto **AG**. 46: Conn-o-Sax **TB**; Conn tenor **GW**. 47: Conn alto **WG**; Conn tenor **GA**. 50: Conn alto **BI**; Grafton alto **BI**. 51: King alto **AG**. 53: Selmer alto **AG**. 55: Selmer alto **WG**. 56: Selmer tenor **AG**. 57: Selmer tenor **BI**; Selmer soprano **BI**. 64: Grafton alto **TB**. 65: King Saxello **TB**. 68: Selmer tenor **AG**. 72: Couesnon alto **WG**. 75: Martin baritone **AG**. 77: Conn tenor **BI**; King tenor **AG**. 79: Selmer alto **BI**. 87: Yamaha alto **BI**. 92: Conn alto **JM**.

Principal photography was by Miki Slingsby.

Existing photographs were supplied by the following (number indicates page). British Film Institute: Richard 79 small. Island Records: Buster 83. Redfern's (BW=Bob Willoughby; CS=Chuck Stewart; DR=David Redfern; LM=Leon Morris; MJ=Max Jones; MO=Michael Ochs; PB=Paul Bergen; WG=William Gottlieb): Bolden 11 (MJ); Oliver 11 (MJ); Beiderbecke 12 (MJ); Rhythm Jugglers 13 (MJ); Wolverines 13 (MO); Armstrong 16 (Dave Bennett); Hot Five 16 (MJ); Basie 17 (MO); Teagarden 17 (MO); Gillespie top 20 (WG), bottom 20 (DR); Brown 21 (CS); Davis 24 (BW), 25 (DR); Barker 29 (DR); Hawkins 38 (WG); Bechet 39 (WG); Parker 51 (MO); Webster 54 (DR); Rollins 56 (DR); Adderley 60 (MO); Coltrane 61 (CS); Coleman 62 (MO); Shepp 64 (LM); Kirk 65 (DR); Osby 68; Brecker 68 (Stephen Engler); Braxton 69; Redman 69 (PB); Garbarek 69 (Fin Costello); Jordan 72/3 (WG), 73 (MO); McNeely 73 (BW); Charles 76 (MO); Haley 76 (DR); Curtis 78 (Gai Terrell); Richard 79 large (Sigi E. Loch); Sinatra 82 (BW); Redding 83 (MO); Walker 83 (DR); Skatellites 83 (DR); Parker 86 (PB); Wesley 86 (LM); Clemons 87 (Donna Santisi); EW&F 87 (A. Dutler). Sotheby's: Martin trumpet 20; Couesnon trumpet 82. Al Stricklin: Wills 72.

Other illustrated items including patents, catalogues, brochures, magazines, advertisements, record sleeves, labels and photographs came from the collections of: Tony Bacon; Balafon; Tony Bingham; Alex Garnett; Willie Garnett; Dave Gelly; *The Music Trades*; The National Jazz Foundation Archive (Loughton, England); Paul Trynka; United Musical Instruments. These heavenly objects were brought to earth through the lens of Miki Slingsby.

QUOTATION sources are generally acknowledged where they occur in the text, except the introductory quotations on page 5: Jaap Kool from his book *Das Saxophon* (1931); Louis Armstrong from his book *Swing That Music* (1936); Miles Davis from an interview in *Down Beat* magazine (1984); Stan Getz from the sleevenote to his album *Another World* (1978) quoted in Donald Maggin's Getz biography; John Coltrane from a piece in *Down Beat* magazine (1960).

THANK YOU to: John R. Adams (United Musical Instruments); Kenny Baker; Rowan S. Baker (Covent Garden Stamp Shop); Dr. Margaret Downie Banks (Shrine To Music Museum); Guy Barker; Tony Bingham; Julie Bowie; Gordon Cherry; Paul Cohen (*Saxophone Journal*); Jason DuMars; Niles Eldredge; Wally Evans (Barnes & Mullins Ltd); Hugh Fairbairn (Phil Parker Ltd); Digby Fairweather; Stan Garber (Selmer Company Inc US); Alex Garnett; Willie Garnett (Garnett Woodwind); Mike Gaze; Dave Gelly; Lori A. Getzen (Getzen Company Inc); Ralph J. Jones; Bharath Karia (Vincent Bach International Ltd); Lars Kirsmer (Music Trader); Randall Kremer (Smithsonian Institution); Ian Lewington (Bill Lewington Ltd); Brian T. Majeski (*The Music Trades*); Roger Manners (Yamaha Corp Japan); Jacquie Martin; David Mason; Stephen Maycock (Sotheby's London); Thomas Meacham; Dave Monette (David G. Monette Corp); David Nathan (National Jazz Foundation Archive); Odile Noel; Jan Osman (Boosey & Hawkes Musical Instruments Ltd); Brian Priestley; Phil Richardson; Alan Rogan; Patrick Selmer (Henri Selmer Paris); David Seville (Yamaha-Kemble Music UK Ltd); Daniel M. Shideler (United Musical Instruments); Sally Stockwell; David Surber (G. Leblanc Corp); Paul Trynka; Jerry Uwins (*Music Business*); Derek Watkins; Christopher Calicchio Weik (Calicchio); John Welton (Redfern's); Gretchen Willoughby (David G. Monette Corp).

SAX & BRASS DIRECTORY We would like to send special thanks to the following individuals who helped considerably in our compilation of information for the Sax & Brass Directory: Dr. Margaret Downie Banks at the Shrine To Music Museum (for her exhaustive research into Conn; you can visit Dr. Banks's Conn-related website at www.usd.edu/~m.banks/CONTENT.html); Paul Cohen (for phone discussions of historical matters, and whose excellent and long-running "Vintage Saxophones Revisited" column in *Saxophone Journal* helped with our Buescher, Conn, Grafton, King and Selmer histories); Jason DuMars (for encouragement at an early stage; visit Mr. DuMars' International Saxophone Home Page at www.saxophone.org); Niles Eldredge (for sharing his Besson historical and serial number information by allowing us access to his unpublished *Besson Bell Signatures: Towards A More Accurate Chronology*); the late Wally Horwood (for his excellent Sax biography, and his fine article on Grafton in *Clarinet & Saxophone*);

Richard R. Ingham (for saxophone insight and keen photocopier service); Ralph J. Jones (serial numbers for Besson and model numbers for Conn; you can visit Mr. Jones's Brass Resources website at www.whc.net/rjones/brassrsc.html); Lars Kirsmer at Music Trader (help with serial numbers for Benge, Boosey & Hawkes, Bueschar/Bundy, Buffet Crampon, Conn, Holton, King, Olds, Reynolds, Schilke, and Selmer trumpets; you can visit Mr. Kirsmer's Music Trader website at www.musictrader.com); Tom Meacham (for Conn model number information); Rob Stewart (for Conn model number information).

BIBLIOGRAPHY

Louis Armstrong *Swing That Music* (DaCapo 1936); Steve Barrow & Peter Dalton *Reggae: The Rough Guide* (Rough Guides 1997); Margaret Downie Banks *Elkhart's Brass Roots* (Shrine To Music Museum 1994); James Brown with Bruce Tucker *James Brown: The Godfather Of Soul* (Sidgwick & Jackson 1987); Ian Carr, Digby Fairweather, Brian Priestley *Jazz: The Essential Companion* (Paladin 1987); Ian Carr, Digby Fairweather, Brian Priestley *Jazz: The Rough Guide* (Rough Guides 1995); John Chilton *Let The Good Times Roll: The Story of Louis Jordan and his Music* (Michigan American Music 1994); John Chilton *Sidney Bechet: The Wizard Of Jazz* (Macmillan 1987); Richard Cook & Brian Morton *The Penguin Guide To Jazz On CD* (Penguin 1996); Miles Davis with Quincy Troupe *Miles: The Autobiography* (Macmillan 1989); Will Friedwald *Sinatra! The Song Is You: A Singer's Art* (Scribner 1995); Dizzy Gillespie with Al Fraser *Dizzy: To Be Or Not To Bop* (W.H. Allen 1979); Robert Gottlieb (ed) *Reading Jazz: A Gathering of Autobiography, Reportage and Criticism from 1919 to Now* (Bloomsbury 1997); Lawrence Gwozdz *Das Saxophon: The Saxophone, an English Translation of Jaap Kool's Work* (Egon 1987); Phil Hardy & Dave Laing *The Faber Companion To 20th Century Popular Music* (Faber & Faber 1990); Wally Horwood *Adolphe Sax 1814-1894: His Life and Legacy* (Bramley 1980); Terry Hounsome *Rock Record 7: Directory of Albums and Musicians* (Record Researcher 1997); Barry Kernfeld (ed) *The New Grove Dictionary Of Jazz* (Macmillan 1994); Jaap Kool *Das Saxophon* (Weber 1931); Colin Lewis *The Guinness Encyclopedia Of Popular Music* (Guinness 1992); Paul Lindemeyer *Celebrating The Saxophone* (Hearst 1996); John Littweiler *Ornette Coleman: The Harmolodic Life* (Morow 1992); Donald L. Maggin *Stan Getz: A Life In Jazz* (Morrow 1996); The Music Trades *The Purchaser's Guide To The Music Industries 1998* (The Music Trades Corp 1998); Stanley Sadie (ed) *The New Grove Dictionary Of Musical Instruments* (Macmillan 1984); Richard M. Sudhalter et al *Bix, Man And Legend* (Arlington House 1974); Charles R. Townsend *San Antonio Rose: The Life and Music of Bob Wills* (University of Illinois Press 1976); Ken Vail *Miles' Diary: The Life of Miles Davis 1947-1961* (Sanctuary 1996).

We also consulted a number of back issues of the following magazines: *Clarinet & Saxophone*; *Crescendo*; *Disc International*; *Down Beat*; *Melody Maker*; *Metronome*; *The Music Trades*; *Rhythm*; *Saxophone Journal*.

You must stir it and stump it,
And blow your own trumpet,
Or trust me, you haven't a chance.
(W.S. Gilbert, 1887)